Mastery and Depth in Primary Mathematics

The UK National Curriculum is clear about the importance of reasoning and problem-solving in mathematics. *Mastery and Depth in Primary Mathematics* aims to support trainee and established teachers to embed mathematical thinking into their lessons. The authors focus on practical and actionable ways that primary teachers can develop their children's mathematical thinking, reasoning and problem-solving: ideas which are at the heart of the UK National Curriculum.

Covering a range of areas in mathematical thinking such as reasoning, problem-solving and pattern-spotting, as well as systematic and investigative thinking, each chapter provides clear examples of how teachers can make small, manageable 'rich tweaks' to their existing lessons to increase the opportunities for children to develop their mathematical thinking. Teachers will be able to dip into the book and find inspiration and ideas that they can use immediately and, importantly, develop a set of principles and skills which will enable them to take any mathematical activity and tweak it to develop their pupils' thinking skills.

This practical guide will be invaluable to all trainee teachers and early-career teachers that wish to enhance their primary mathematics teaching.

Fay Lewis, after completing her PhD and PGCE, worked as a teacher in primary schools in Yorkshire, Somerset and Bristol for almost 15 years. She now works at the University of the West of England, where she heads up the Master in Education programme and teaches all things related to science, technology, engineering, and mathematics to undergraduate and postgraduate student primary school teachers.

Amanda Wilkinson, prior to becoming a teacher educator, worked for several years as a primary teacher in Manchester and Oxfordshire. During this time, she trained to become a specialist mathematics teacher, became a senior leader and worked part-time as a mathematics consultant. Since then, she has worked as a senior lecturer in primary mathematics, first for Oxford Brookes University and then for the University of the West of England in Bristol.

Marcus Witt began his teaching career in the hills of South India, teaching in an international school before moving to a school in rural Kentucky and then completing his PGCE in the UK. After several years teaching in primary schools, he moved to teacher education and now works at the University of the West of England, helping train the next generation of primary school teachers.

Mastery and Depth in Primary Mathematics

Enriching Children's Mathematical Thinking

Fay Lewis, Amanda Wilkinson
and Marcus Witt

LONDON AND NEW YORK

Cover image: © Getty Images

First published 2022
by Routledge
4 Park Square, Milton Park, Abingdon, Oxon OX14 4RN

and by Routledge
605 Third Avenue, New York, NY 10158

Routledge is an imprint of the Taylor & Francis Group, an informa business

© 2022 Fay Lewis, Amanda Wilkinson and Marcus Witt

The right of Fay Lewis, Amanda Wilkinson and Marcus Witt to be identified as authors of this work has been asserted in accordance with sections 77 and 78 of the Copyright, Designs and Patents Act 1988.

All rights reserved. No part of this book may be reprinted or reproduced or utilised in any form or by any electronic, mechanical, or other means, now known or hereafter invented, including photocopying and recording, or in any information storage or retrieval system, without permission in writing from the publishers.

Trademark notice: Product or corporate names may be trademarks or registered trademarks, and are used only for identification and explanation without intent to infringe.

British Library Cataloguing-in-Publication Data
A catalogue record for this book is available from the British Library

Library of Congress Cataloging-in-Publication Data
Names: Lewis, Fay (College teacher), author. | Wilkinson, Amanda
   (Mathematics educator), author. | Witt, Marcus, author.
Title: Mastery and depth in primary mathematics : enriching children's
   mathematical thinking / Fay Lewis, Amanda Wilkinson, and Marcus Witt.
Description: Milton Park, Abingdon, Oxon ; New York, NY : Routledge,
   2022. | Includes bibliographical references and index.
Identifiers: LCCN 2021034716 | ISBN 9780367407445 (hardback) |
   ISBN 9780367407452 (paperback) | ISBN 9780367808860 (ebook)
Subjects: LCSH: Mathematics—Study and teaching (Primary)—Great Britain.
Classification: LCC QA135.6 .L496 2022 | DDC 372.7—dc23/eng/20211014
LC record available at https://lccn.loc.gov/2021034716

ISBN: 978-0-367-40744-5 (hbk)
ISBN: 978-0-367-40745-2 (pbk)
ISBN: 978-0-367-80886-0 (ebk)

DOI: 10.4324/9780367808860

Typeset in Palatino
by Apex CoVantage, LLC

Contents

Introduction 1

1 The national curriculum, 'mastery', depth and making sense of the problem at the heart of primary mathematics teaching. 7

2 Reasoning with calculations 21

3 Reasoning in geometry and statistics 41

4 Problem-solving 63

5 Patterns and variation 85

6 Mathematical investigations, systematic thinking and finding all the possibilities 109

7 Planning for mathematical thinking 131

Conclusion 143

Index 145

Introduction

There are many excellent books available which will support you with your teaching of primary mathematics. They are mostly structured around the different areas of the primary mathematics curriculum and have sections on number, calculation, geometry, measures and the like. The best of them are fantastic resources to support you with the development of your subject knowledge and pedagogical knowledge and help you with planning maths lessons. You may therefore be wondering why there is a need for this book. How is this book different from others?

We hope that this book addresses a different need. The introduction to the National Curriculum makes it clear that children who grasp concepts easily should have their mathematical experience deepened and enriched. The widespread adoption of a 'mastery' approach to teaching mathematics has led to a welcome focus on the depth of children's mathematical thinking and the need for teachers to design tasks and activities which develop children's mathematical thinking skills, as well as their knowledge and understanding of mathematical concepts. However, the curriculum document provides limited guidance about how this might be done.

This book aims to support pre-service (trainee) teachers and Early Career Teachers (ECT), who wish to incorporate more mathematical thinking into their lessons but are unsure about how to do this.

The structure of the book

Rather than organise the book around the different areas of the primary mathematics curriculum, we have chosen to devote chapters to particular areas of mathematical thinking. We offer the idea of 'rich tweaks', ways of making subtle, and often minimal, changes to the activities that you have planned or the way that you frame the activity or ask questions which will significantly increase the opportunities for children to engage in deep mathematical thinking. The following section explores each of the subsequent eight chapters in a little more detail. There is no need to read the chapters in order; if you are particularly interested in developing the children's skills in investigative thinking, you can jump straight into the relevant chapter.

Chapter 1 aims to take an overview of what deep mathematical thinking might 'look like' and explores ideas such as 'mastery' and depth, the notion of 'low-threshold, high-ceiling' activities and some 'big ideas' in mathematics teaching, as outlined by the Association of Teachers of Mathematics.

In Chapter 2, we look at ways of developing children's mathematical reasoning in and through calculation. It is possible to become very procedural when teaching calculations, focusing solely on enabling the children to perform the algorithms (e.g. $45 \times 2 = 90, 3 + 7 = 10$). However, by focusing too much on answers and algorithms, we miss an opportunity to develop the children's reasoning. In this chapter, we introduce the idea of a 'rich tweak', a way of taking something relatively 'standard' and straightforward, such as an abstract calculation, and tweaking it so that the children's reasoning skills are developed. We demonstrate how some very simple rich tweaks to the ways calculations are presented can significantly deepen the children's reasoning about them.

One of our motivations for writing this book is the belief that mathematical thinking and reasoning can be promoted in all areas of maths. With this in mind, in Chapter 3, we look at the areas of geometry and statistics, areas which haven't always been so closely associated with the idea of mathematical thinking. How can teachers develop children's thinking in area and perimeter or graphs? It's easier than you might think, and with a few rich tweaks, we will hopefully show you how.

Chapter 4 looks specifically at problem-solving and how to go about helping children to develop their skills in this area of mathematics. Problem solving is notoriously difficult to teach, so much so that many teachers can struggle with this. We suggest some ways in which you can support children as they work on problems without ending up doing too much for them. We can consider how we can break down the problem, help the children really 'see' what the maths is and suggest ways of developing the children's independence and resilience when solving problems.

In the fifth chapter, we really try to dig deep into many of Barclay and Barnes's 'Big Ideas'. How can we encourage children to pattern spot or develop an understanding of how to generalise? We look at the idea of mathematical proof and what are suitable activities for the primary school classroom. Children also need to be encouraged to predict and hypothesise in maths as well as science, so we introduce some ideas about how to encourage this too.

Mathematical investigations are the subject of Chapter 6. This is another area of maths which can be underrepresented in the classroom. Yet this is a part of the mathematics curriculum that can be rich in opportunities for reasoning and thinking. Given the chance to explore and investigate, children can be encouraged to share their thinking and develop their reasoning all without the need to find the 'right' answer immediately. We begin this chapter by taking you through a simple maths investigation (don't panic, there is no difficult maths involved, and you can use a calculator if you need to), highlighting some of the key mathematical thinking skills that are prompted by the investigation. We then take you into two maths classrooms to explore how similar investigations can be tweaked to provide a rich context for the development of mathematical thinking.

In Chapter 7, we think about how to use your planning to help you to integrate reasoning into your teaching. What areas need to be thought about to maximise the potential for maths lessons to develop reasoning? What connects many of these chapters together is the idea that reasoning and mathematical thinking are not something extra or a 'bolt on' to everyday maths learning in the classroom. A guiding principle of this book is to demonstrate that reasoning can be integrated into teaching and that, with a few 'rich tweaks', developed through the curriculum rather than as an extra to it.

We finally conclude by pulling all these ideas together and suggesting some ways forward.

How to use this book

As mentioned earlier, we have used the idea of 'rich tweaks' throughout this book. A rich tweak is a small change to an existing activity which significantly increases the opportunities for mathematical thinking in the activity. We appreciate that teachers are hugely busy, so we have tried to design our 'rich tweaks' so that they do not require a lot of additional planning time (and, in many cases, require less planning time) but have a big impact. The rich tweaks that we suggest are intended to be examples to prompt further thinking. Hopefully you will think of rich tweaks of your own and will be able to improve on the ones we suggest.

Many of the chapters contain glimpses of some of these rich tweaks being applied in classrooms so that you get a sense of what they 'look like' and how children may respond to them. In these sections, we have tried to step back from the description of what is happening in the classroom to consider some of the teaching strategies that are being used to make the rich tweaks more effective.

The end of most chapters contains a list of further activities and related rich tweaks to try with your class. We do encourage you to give some of these things a try and see how possible it is, with a little practice, to embed mathematical thinking into your maths lessons without compromising coverage of the essential content.

All the authors of the book are enthusiastic about getting all children thinking mathematically as part of their daily mathematics experience in school. We hope you find the book accessible and interesting, and that the ideas in it will help you add even more mathematical colour and spice to your lessons.

1
The national curriculum, 'mastery', depth and making sense of the problem at the heart of primary mathematics teaching

Figure 1.1

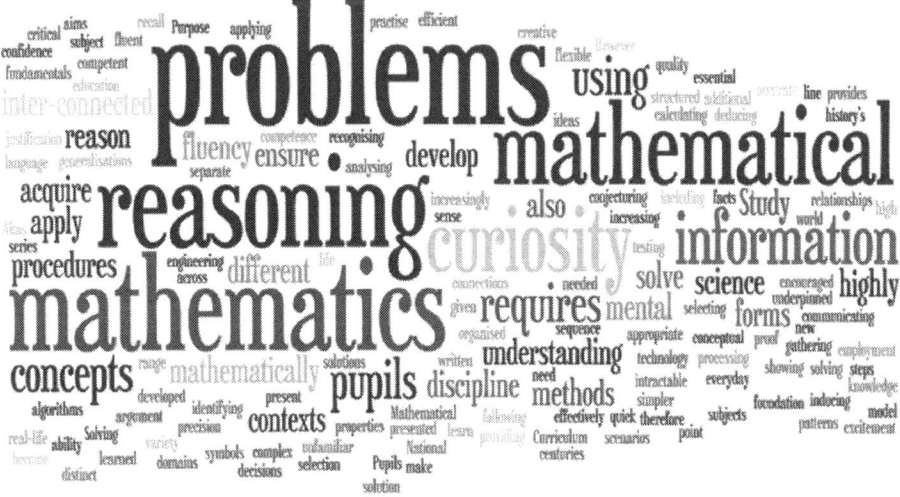

The problem

The picture in Figure 1.1 is a summary of the first four pages of the Primary National Curriculum for Mathematics. The size of each word reflects the number of times that word is mentioned.

DOI: 10.4324/9780367808860-2

We include this here, at the start of the book, because we think that it illustrates one of the fundamental difficulties that teachers, like you, have with using the curriculum document.

The National Curriculum for primary mathematics (DfE, 2013) has, at its heart, a problem for pre-service and Early Career mathematics teachers. The introductory pages state clearly the vision and aspiration for a deep and comprehensive mathematics education for children up to the age of 11. Such an education should include opportunities to increase fluency, to develop reasoning in mathematics and to engage in problem-solving. The curriculum document reminds teachers that children need to engage with 'rich and sophisticated problems' and to make connections between mathematics and other areas of the curriculum. **However, and here's the problem, the subsequent forty-three pages of the document provide little, or no guidance to teachers about how to live up to these ideals.** There is a lot of guidance about the content of the curriculum, but very little about how new teachers can incorporate the need to develop fluency, reasoning and problem-solving skills into their teaching so that the children are both covering the required content and developing those skills. The Advisory Committee on Mathematics Education, in a publication in 2014, acknowledged the challenges faced by teachers implementing the (then) 'new' National Curriculum and saw 'a need to develop a broad understanding of core curricular aims amongst teachers' (p. 2),

If you are training to become a primary school teacher or are newly or recently qualified or are a more experienced teacher who wishes to develop your maths teaching further, we hope that this book will be of interest to you. The aim of this book is to support you to be able to achieve the aims of the National Curriculum document by suggesting ways in which mathematical skills (such as reasoning and problem-solving) might be embedded into your lessons. This is no easy task but one that is essential if children in primary classrooms are to have an experience of mathematics that is as rich as the one suggested in the first four pages of the curriculum document. We begin with a consideration of the context in which these wider mathematical skills are being taught.

Mastery

The Programme of International Student Assessment (PISA) assesses 15-year-old children from a variety of countries (or other jurisdictions) around the world with a view to providing an international comparison of mathematics achievement. This is done every three years, with the results usually published the year after the data is collected. The results of the 2012 data (published in 2013) showed the city of Shanghai clearly outperforming all other countries or jurisdictions. In 2014, the UK government launched a number of 'Maths Hubs' around the country, with the intention to disseminate best practices in mathematics teaching. As part of this, an exchange programme with Shanghai was established in which UK teachers went to Shanghai to observe teaching and Chinese teachers came to the UK to share ideas and teach demonstration lessons.

From this exchange programme, and from looking at curriculum documents from other high-performing countries, the notion of maths 'mastery' arose. This has now become part of the 'conversation' about good practice in primary mathematics and is relevant to the problem identified earlier.

The National Centre for Excellence in the Teaching of Mathematics (NCETM), an organisation, which has enthusiastically supported the introduction of 'mastery' principles into UK classrooms has published what it considers to be the five underpinning ideas in 'mastery' (NCETM, 2015). The five principles are as follows:

- Coherence (breaking new learning up into a series of small but logically connected smaller steps)
- Representation and Structure (the use in lessons of different representations to illustrate and expose underlying mathematical structures and concepts)

- Mathematical Thinking (the importance of children gaining more than an ability to carry out processes, or procedures, but that they understand why they are doing so. This has echoes Skemp's (1976) ideas about instrumental and relational understanding.
- Fluency (children should have quick and accurate recall of number facts but should also be able to move fluently and flexibly between different representations of the maths and mathematical contexts)
- Variation (attention is given to the sequencing of the different lessons and the way that examples and questions are organised so that children's attention is focused on what changes [varies] and what stays the same. Through this attention, the underlying mathematical structure is made clearer)

The NCETM has also published a number of guides to 'mastery' (Askew et al., 2015) which explore what 'mastery' might look like in different year groups. These publications also provide some guidance as we try to embed their ideas into our lessons. The guides suggest that a child has mastered a mathematical concept if they are able to explain it in their own words, give examples and counter-examples to illustrate it, represent it in a variety of ways, apply it to different contexts and problems and make connections between it and other facts or ideas. We refer to these as 'markers of mastery'. Therefore, as we explore ways to support you in embedding ideas about mastery into your lessons, we consider how you might create opportunities for children to exhibit (and therefore to develop) some of the 'markers of mastery' outlined earlier.

Although 'mastery' is not mentioned explicitly in the National Curriculum, many of the principles outlined earlier are present in the picture of mathematics painted in its first few pages. Therefore, as we come to think about ways to embed some of the National Curriculum ideals into mathematics teaching, we draw on ideas about mastery as presented by the NCETM.

Depth – enrichment rather than acceleration

Drury (2018) suggests that one of the key ideas underpinning mastery is the belief that all children are able to understand and do mathematics, given sufficient time. She states (p. 1) 'to teach for mastery is to teach with the highest expectation for every learner, so that their understanding is deepened'. She further breaks down the idea of 'depth' into three 'dimensions of depth'. These are the deepening of conceptual understanding by seeing connections between concepts and between different representations of concepts, encouraging children to think like mathematicians by seeing patterns and rules, posing and answering mathematical questions and developing mathematical communication skills. This is again echoed in some of the ideas in the first part of the National Curriculum, which states:

> Pupils who grasp concepts rapidly should be challenged through rich and sophisticated problems before any acceleration through new content. Those pupils who are not sufficiently fluent with earlier material should consolidate their understanding, including through additional practice, before moving on.
>
> (p. 3)

There is agreement that children should be challenged to develop a deep understanding of the mathematical concepts they are learning before they are moved to new ideas. While this aim is very welcome (as is the shift from an approach that advocated 'acceleration' through the curriculum), it presents pre-service or Early Career teachers with a problem. Where are these 'rich and sophisticated' problems? How can they be incorporated into lessons so that the children described previously are challenged in mathematics lessons and are developing the depth of understanding that Drury and the National Curriculum seem to demand?

Ideas to help solve 'the problem'

The good news is that you are not alone in trying to find ways to enable your children to have the kind of mathematical experiences imagined by the National Curriculum and by those advocating a 'mastery' approach to mathematical learning. In this next section, we consider some of the places (other than the rest of this book) where you could look for inspiration and some of the key principles which inform the suggestions that we make in the subsequent chapters of the book.

Nrich (see https://nrich.maths.org/) is an organisation, which seeks explicitly to enrich and deepen children's mathematical experiences. It contains a huge number of rich tasks, designed with problem-solving and deepening experience in mind. However, your job is to do a little more than hunt around for other people's lesson ideas. While we thoroughly endorse everything that Nrich does and stands for, we want you to be able to make 'rich tweaks' to existing tasks or activities so as to deepen your pupils' mathematical experience. We would also like you to be able to design your own rich tasks so that you are able to embed them successfully into your lessons. We will therefore look at some of the key principles behind the Nrich tasks.

One of the key principles, which informs many of the Nrich tasks, is the idea of 'low threshold, high ceiling' (LTHC). The Nrich team (2013) sum up LTHC as meaning that 'everyone can get started, everyone can get stuck.' We understand this to mean that the task has an easy entry point so that all learners, almost irrespective of their current mathematical understanding, can make a start on the task. Lee and Johnson-Wilder (2018) suggest that developing resilience when doing mathematics is an important part of learning. We feel that learners are more likely to persist with a task if they have already experienced some success with it. Indeed, several writers (Barton, 2018) suggest that the relationship between mathematical success and motivation is bidirectional and that success may be a stronger predictor of motivation than motivation is of success. Designing tasks that have an easy entry point (low threshold) will increase the likelihood that your learners will persist. The notion that 'everyone can get stuck' is not intended to be off-putting. The Nrich Team (2013) note that getting stuck (and then getting unstuck) develops resilience and that allowing children to experience this as part of their mathematical education normalises it.

An analogy that many teachers find useful here is James Nottingham's (2017) 'Learning Pit'. This encourages children to 'get in the pit' and then get out again, thus building resilience in their mathematical approach. Children can often find encouragement when they are told it's okay, in fact it is desirable, to get things wrong and not be sure what to do next. Put more simply, this is the idea of being stuck on a problem. The Learning Pit actually encourages children to recognise when they are in this stuck state and, to some extent, celebrate it. When children recognise that they are stuck in the pit, they can then consider what tools they have to get out of the pit. They can also see that their current situation is an important part of learning. They then might ask themselves the question, 'How did I get out of this last time? Or 'Where can I find resources to help?' Nottingham (2017) argues that all of this can not only develop the children resilience but also lead to a deeper more permanent level of learning.

For many children, the idea of mathematical learning is that the teacher smooths the path for them to the point that they never experience any difficulties or 'bumps in the road'. A feature of these LTHC tasks is that there is no fixed end-point but that different children can take them in different directions and may reach different stopping points, or points at which they get stuck. As we consider ways to embed opportunities to embed mathematical thinking skills (see p. 1) into your maths lessons, we will return to ideas about LTHC.

The Nrich Team (2013) note that some tasks may appear to be mathematically 'low threshold' but have other barriers, possibly psychological ones, to getting started. If a child has the required amount of mathematical understanding to begin a task but feels overwhelmed by the context or the structure of the task, they may feel unable to begin. They note that 'some problems may require a very basic understanding of the mathematical content to solve, and yet still be extremely challenging'. In designing tasks that are genuinely LTHC, we need to consider more than the mathematical content of the task. In considering what LTHC tasks might 'look like' as you seek to create an LTHC classroom, the Nrich team emphasise the need for questions that draw learners' attention to what is the same and what is different and to encourage learners to represent their mathematical thinking in different ways. The teacher might then ask specific children, who have chosen to represent their thinking differently from each other, to show and explain their thinking to the rest of the children. Encouraging the asking of questions as a result of these explanations might further encourage learners to explore avenues of interest for themselves.

'Big ideas' in primary mathematics teaching

Barclay and Barnes (2013) identified a number of 'big ideas' in primary mathematics teaching. Their aim in identifying them was to enable teachers and children to 'develop connection and coherence in a curriculum which comprises micro-level objectives' (p. 19). This seems very much in line with the aims of this book, namely to enable you to embed opportunities for children to engage in 'bigger' mathematical thinking into your lessons. Their 'big ideas' are as follows:

> Pattern and structure. The inherent structure in mathematics gives rise to patterns, which make prediction and mathematical hypothesis possible (we explore these ideas in more detail in later chapters). Looking for, seeing and using patterns is a way of encouraging children to see the underlying structure in mathematics and to move beyond the accomplishment of micro-objectives into 'bigger' mathematical thinking.

Representation. This links very clearly to the NCETM's concept of 'mastery' and to the ideas presented by the Nrich team about encouraging children to represent their thinking in a variety of ways.

Logic and Proof. There can be no mathematical reasoning without logic. Constructing tasks which engage children in reasoning will be a significant part of this book. While proof may seem mathematically beyond the reach of children in primary school, Barnes and Barclay argue that all children can engage in mathematical proof at some level.

Equivalence. Haylock (2018) suggests that asking children to focus on what is the same and what is different is an excellent way of encouraging them to see the mathematics beyond the procedural.

Divergent Thinking. Barclay and Barnes characterise this 'big idea' as the development of approaches to solve mathematical problems. Initially, they gave this 'big idea' the title 'problem solving' but changed it to encompass some of the mathematical thinking skills that are inherent in solving mathematical problems, namely forming and testing conjectures and moving beyond a simple step-by-step process for solving problems.

Generality. Moving on from seeing patterns is the idea that children should use them to make predictions about what will happen in the future and therefore whether some general conclusions can be drawn.

Communication. Barclay and Barnes pay particular attention to the importance of classroom talk and learners posing mathematical questions (which echoes Drury's notion of children developing a depth of understanding through developing their mathematical communication skills).

Resilience. This 'big idea' is somewhat different from the others in that it is not an inherently mathematical idea but is more of a disposition towards the learning of the subject. The authors note that resilience can have both a cognitive and an affective (emotional) element.

Embedding mathematical thinking into lessons

All these lists of 'big ideas' and principles for mastery teaching may seem rather overwhelming initially. There is an awful lot to plan into maths lessons, in addition to covering the objectives in the National Curriculum. And yet, all these ideas and aspirations seem to be an inherent part of a deep and comprehensive primary mathematics education and therefore well worth the effort of embedding them into classroom activities and tasks. As we have said, the aim of this book is to support you in embedding opportunities for children to engage in this kind of mathematical thinking into your lessons. Try not to be overwhelmed by all the possible mathematical thinking that you could embed into every lesson. As Back et al., 2013 say,

> [h]uman nutrition is immensely complicated, yet most of us believe that if we eat a sensible amount of a wide variety of foods, our bodies will naturally take the nutrients they need in the appropriate amounts. To try to plan for every vitamin, for example by giving each one separately, would be impossibly complex, and mirrors for me what happens when micro-learning objectives assume central importance in the classroom. If I offer learners a rich variety of mathematical experiences, perhaps I should trust them to take what they need from each in the quantities that they can handle at that time?
>
> (p. 6)

So, don't worry. Take heart from the fact that, if you can embed some of the ideas we discuss into some of your lessons, your learners will be receiving a much deeper and more interesting mathematics education than if you don't.

This book is full of examples and case studies, and as such, it will hopefully be a rich source of ideas and activities for your own teaching. The issue with practical examples, however, is they can be very specific to a particular age group, or area of mathematics and can therefore feel that they are not always directly relevant to your own specific situation. The model shown in Figure 1.2 can be a useful way of thinking about any activity that we suggest in this book. At first you might think that's a good idea (hopefully), but that it's not relevant to the age group you teach. However, if you reflect further, you could adapt the idea to your class. Next you might think that you can change the idea so it can use it in a wholly different area of mathematics. Finally you might consider what the underlying pedagogy is and how you might use this in a broader sense in your teaching.

Figure 1.2

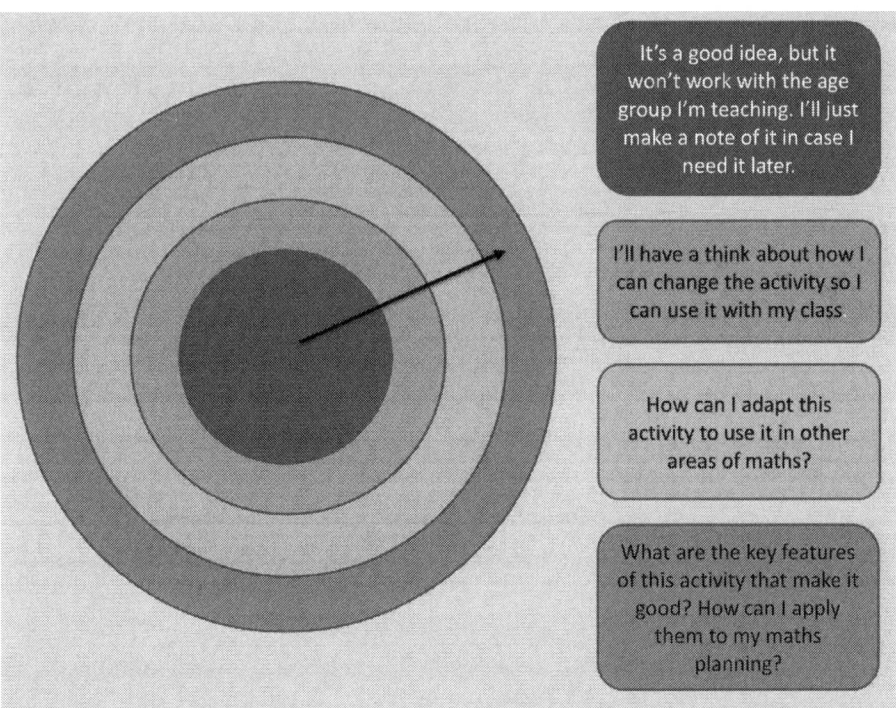

For example, take the 'guess the shape' activity in Chapter 3, where a shape is slowly revealed and the children are encouraged to give their reasons why it might be one shape or another. How might this be used with another age group of children? What support or adjustment would make this more age-appropriate? We might change the shapes or the vocabulary for example. Going further, you might consider how it could work in other areas of mathematics entirely with a few changes? What else can slowly be revealed and children be encouraged to discuss their thinking about it? Can this be applied to a set of numbers or a calculation or, in fact, to any area of maths you happen to be teaching. And finally, you might start to consider what the underlying pedagogies of the activity are. Why do they work as a way of transforming knowledge from your understanding to the children?

This way of thinking about activities and ideas is something that, perhaps unconsciously, experienced teachers do all the time. Taking ideas and adapting them is both a way of building your repertoire of teaching approaches as well as a way of learning new ideas to refresh your own teaching. No pedagogic ideas are copyrighted, in fact, taking ideas and adapting them is one of the ways that the teaching profession moves forward and develops.

References

Advisory Committee on Mathematics Education (ACME). (2014) *The National Curriculum*. Maths Snapshots. Available from: www.acme-uk.org/media/20272/mathscurriculum.pdf (Accessed: 10 August 2020).

Askew, M., Bishop, S., Christie, C., Eaton, S., Griffin, P. and Morgan, D. (2015) *Teaching for Mastery. Questions, Tasks and Activities to Support Assessment*. Oxford: Oxford University Press.

Back, J., Foster, C., Tomalin, J., Mason, J., Swan, M. and Watson, A. (2013) Tasks and their place in mathematical teaching and learning. *Mathematics Teaching*, 232, pp. 6–8. Available from: www.foster77.co.uk/ATM-MT232-06-08.pdf (Accessed: 10 August 2020).

Barclay, N. and Barnes, A. (2013) Big Ideas – an idea with primary potential. *Mathematics Teaching*, 232, pp. 19–21.

Available from: www.atm.org.uk/write/MediaUploads/Resources/Big_Ideas.pdf (Accessed: 10 August 2020).

Barton, C. (2018) *How I Wish I'd Taught Maths*. Woodbridge: John Catt Educational.

Department for Education. (2013) *The National Curriculum in England: Key Stages 1 and 2 Framework Document*. Available from: www.gov.uk/government/publications/national-curriculum-in-england-primary-curriculum (Accessed: 10 August 2020).

Drury, H. (2018) *How to Teach Mathematics for Mastery*. Oxford: Oxford University Press.

Haylock, D. (2018) *Mathematics Explained for Primary Teachers* (6th Edition). London: Sage.

Lee, C. and Johnson-Wilder, S. (2018) *Getting Into and Staying in the Growth Zone*. Available from: https://nrich.maths.org/13491

NCETM. (2015) *Five Big Ideas for Teaching Mastery*. Available from: www.ncetm.org.uk/teaching-for-mastery/mastery-explained/five-big-ideas-in-teaching-for-mastery/ (Accessed: 10 August 2020).

Nottingham, J. (2017) *The Learning Challenge*. London: Sage.

Nrich Team. (2013) *Low Threshold High Ceiling: An Introduction*. Available from: https://nrich.maths.org/10345 (Accessed: 10 August 2020).

Skemp, R. R. (1976) Relational understanding and instrumental understanding. *Mathematics Teaching*, 77, pp. 20–26.

2
Reasoning with calculations

Chapter overview

In this chapter, we aim to explore ways of developing children's reasoning through calculation. We explore how you can make simple 'rich tweaks' to the kinds of calculations that your children will be doing as a matter of course. These tweaks will, we hope, provide them with greater opportunities to develop their reasoning skills in the context of calculation and will deepen their understanding of the different calculations they encounter. The chapter contains case studies, which are intended to exemplify some of the suggestions. However, as with all the suggestions in the book, we encourage you to think beyond the specific cases, which are described and consider how you might make a similar 'rich tweak' for your own children.

Much has been written, but much remains to be written about children's mathematical reasoning. It is not the intention of this book to provide a comprehensive review of the literature on this subject. However, there is no doubt of its importance in children's mathematical development. Nunes et al. (2009) provide clear evidence of a causal link between children's mathematical reasoning and their subsequent mathematical development. The National Curriculum for Mathematics (2014) states the following:

> *A high-quality mathematics education therefore provides a foundation for understanding the world, the ability to reason*

mathematically, an appreciation of the beauty and power of mathematics, and a sense of enjoyment and curiosity about the subject.

(p. 3)

However, Christodoulou (2017) is clear that good reasoning (in any subject) is dependent on domain-specific knowledge; it is impossible to reason about shapes without a knowledge and understanding of their properties. Equally, it is impossible to reason about numbers without an understanding of the logical relationships between them and an understanding of the number system (Gilmore et al., 2018). Therefore, we are not suggesting that the ideas and activities discussed in this chapter be done in isolation or with children who have little or no understanding of the number system. We are suggesting that engaging in activities that seek to develop children's reasoning will help both the development of children's reasoning skills and their understanding of the number system and calculation. Nunes et al. (2015) suggest clearly that teaching children to reason mathematically is possible. In the following discussion, we suggest a number of 'rich tweaks' that, we hope, will help you incorporate mathematical reasoning into your lessons involving calculation and numbers.

Rich Tweak 1 – Moving the position of the unknown in calculation questions

Given the importance of reasoning for children's subsequent mathematical development, we recommend incorporating reasoning into children's experiences of calculation once they have a secure understanding of mathematical operations. All children will complete hundreds of calculations during their time in primary school. We suspect that many of them (and certainly a majority of the questions we see on pre-prepared worksheets and in textbooks) are in the following form:

Known (operation) Known = Unknown (e.g. 4 + 8 = ?, or 14 – 5 = ?)

The operation may vary, but the position of the known items and the unknown (the solution to the calculation) is very often in that form, that is the last element in the calculation and following the equals sign. We are going to suggest that by tweaking the calculation to vary the position of the unknown element of the calculation offers opportunities for more mathematical reasoning. Consider the following calculations:

Figure 2.1

7 + 4 = ◼

7 + ◼ = 11

◼ + 4 = 11

Before you read on, we invite you to spend a moment considering the differences between these three calculations in terms of the mathematical demands they make of the children. Are they all equally demanding? Do some of these questions require more reasoning than others? What might the problems be for children tackling these questions using manipulative objects?

What we are suggesting here is that you deliberately vary the position of the unknown in the calculations that you give your children. Try to avoid a situation in which your children only ever see calculations in one form.

Rich Tweak 1 – Case study

Mr Knight inherited a class of children in Year 2 whose only experience with calculations had been doing calculations in the first of the forms given in Figure 2.1. They had become skilled at using manipulative objects to complete the calculations, gathering 7 objects and 4 more and then putting them together to 'make' 11. When questioned about what the symbols in the calculation were asking them to do, they confidently explained that they were putting together 7 and 4 objects to make 11. They were clear that the equality symbol meant 'makes' and came before the answer. It would have been easy to assume that the children had a clear understanding of addition and were competent to move to larger numbers.

However, when presented with calculations in the second form by Mr Knight, many of the children struggled. A number wrote 18 in the empty box, and far fewer of them were able to articulate a clear understanding of what the symbols were requiring them to do (this is a common occurrence in primary classrooms; see Skemp, 1976, for a full discussion). Crucially, their experience prior to this had not really required them to reason about the calculations; they had become used to following a process, which was leading to correct answers but without a deep conceptual understanding (one of the markers of mastery). Mr Knight's use of Rich Tweak 1, the introduction of calculations in the other forms noted in Figure 2.1) caused the children to reason about what the symbols were requiring them to do (i.e. 'What must I add to 7 to get 11?'). Once the children had become fluent with these calculations (and we recommend a mixture of the 3 types of calculation so that the children do not simply revert to learning a process without reasoning), they were introduced to the following, which we will term Rich Tweak 2.

Rich Tweak 2 – Reasoning using the equality symbol

Figure 2.2

☐ = 7 + 4

11 = 7 + ☐

11 = ☐ + 4

Questions in this form provided Mr Knight's children with some additional reasoning problems. We should point out here that we are not advocating that you give the children this kind of calculation without having already taught them the correct meaning of the equals sign (=). Children who think that the equality symbol means 'makes', or 'here comes the answer', will just find these calculations frustrating and confusing. Haylock (2014) is one of many textbooks that give clear explanations of the equality symbol, but briefly, it is important that the children have a clear understanding that the symbol shows simply that what is on one side of the symbol is equal to what is on the other side.

Takeaway

The important message from this first section of the chapter is that it is very important to give the children calculations in a variety of forms. We have just looked at addition, but this works equally well for any of the four operations (addition, subtraction, multiplication and division). From a single calculation here, we now have six possible arrangements, which means that the lucky children in your classroom should have a rich variety of calculations, which will develop their reasoning and understanding of the logical relations between numbers.

Rich Tweak 3 – Varying the unknown in formal written calculations

Later the school, the children will be introduced to more formal written algorithms as the numbers they are calculating become larger and the need for abstract symbols will be greater. This should not prevent you from developing their reasoning about different calculation algorithms and the logical relationships between numbers. Abi, a girl in Year 4 was asked to talk about how she approached the two calculations shown in Figure 2.3.

Figure 2.3

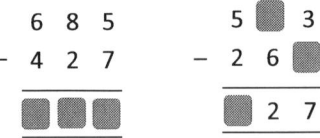

In calculation 1, Abi explained the need to begin at the right-hand side and subtract the ones (units) first. She was unclear as to why she had to begin there but was sure that it was correct to do so. She was also able to explain that she needed to cross out the number in the tens column, reduce it by one and 'move the one over to the ones column and put it in front of the ones already there'. This made the calculation in the ones column possible, and Abi successfully completed the calculation. We have met a number of children like Abi, who are reasonably confident in carrying out multi-digit calculations but whose understanding of what they are doing is not always clear. We suggest that the use of calculations, which require more reasoning (like the second calculation), as well as developing children's reasoning skills about calculation, can act as a good sources of assessment evidence, as they will tend to identify children whose understanding of a particular calculation process is incomplete.

Abi struggled with the second calculation, claiming that it wasn't possible, as 'three take away something can't leave you with seven.' With some encouragement, she was able to see that it might be possible to take one of the tens from the tens column and move it to the ones column, making 13 in total. She was then clear that the missing number would need to be 6 'because you need to take six away from thirteen to leave you with seven.' Abi initially thought that the missing number in the tens column must be 8 but, after some consideration, concluded that 'it must have been 9 to begin with, because we took one away to make the 13'. She was then able to reason her way through the rest of the calculation.

We would argue that implementing Rich Tweak 3 and engaging (albeit in a supported way) with this second calculation caused

Abi to engage in some mathematical reasoning that she would not have had to do, had her experiences of multi-digit subtraction calculations been limited to the first example in Figure 2.3. We would like to reiterate that trying the second calculation without a reasonable degree of fluency (and at least some understanding) of the formal algorithm would have led to nothing but frustration. Deciding when to introduce children to calculations which require more reasoning is a matter of careful timing.

Take-away

A development on moving the position of the unknown in calculations that are presented in a linear fashion is to move the position of the unknown digits in calculations presented in a more 'formal' vertical way.

Rich Tweak 4 – Further developments in reasoning in calculation; more than three elements

We feel that, while some children may see calculations in the forms written in Figure 2.3, they rarely see them in the form shown in Figure 2.4.

Figure 2.4

6 + 9 = 7 + ■

It is essential that young children have a clear understanding of the equal sign, so calculations in this form may reveal gaps in children's understanding of this. Once they have a clear understanding, calculations presented in this form will help develop their reasoning about the logical relations between numbers.

Children may begin by giving the answer 22 to this, as they will see three numbers: two addition symbols and an equal sign. However, a reminder to the children that the equals sign simply means that what is on one side of it is the same as what is on the other side will encourage them to engage in reasoning. Joe approached the calculation by first adding the 6 and the 9 to get 15 and then subtracting 7 to leave 8. If the numbers involved are small and well within the children's calculating capacity, finding the unknown by a process of calculation may be the quickest (and most obvious way). However, consider this calculation:

Figure 2.5

276 + 134 = 277 + ▢

For many children, the calculations needed to find the unknown here are beyond what they could reasonably do mentally and the process of carrying out two quite complicated three-digit formal calculations (276 + 134 and then subtracting the result from 277), may lead them to seek an alternative solution using reasoning. In your questioning here, you may like to draw the children's attention to the different numbers in the calculation and guide them to notice that two of them are very close (i.e. have a difference of one). They may then be able to reason that the missing number must be one less than 134 so that the two sides of the equation balance. This representation may be more helpful to them.

Once the children are familiar with this, there are multiple opportunities to vary the operation involved, the differences between the numbers and the position of the unknown or unknowns. Have a look at and try to work out the unknowns in the following examples:

Figure 2.6

276 − 134 = 277 − ▢

26 × 4 = ▢ × 8

216 ÷ 12 = ▢ ÷ 6

In the examples given in Figure 2.6, the connections are intended to be fairly clear to the children (e.g. 276 and 277 are very close to each other), so the adjustment to the 134 will be a small one (but working out which way to adjust provides opportunities for a lot of reasoning). It would be possible to vary this further. Take the example in Figure 2.7:

Figure 2.7

276 − 134 = 286 − ▇

The adjustment is now 10, and again, the reasoning is about which way to adjust. Before you move on to the rest of the chapter, we invite you to consider the age group you are currently teaching and to compile a couple of calculations in this form (i.e. with two elements on either side of the equality symbol) that you could use with them to cause them to reason more about the nature of particular operations and about the relationships between numbers. Experiment with different operations and with the position of the unknown, the similarity of the numbers on either side of the equality symbol, and so on.

Before we leave this particular idea, consider the calculation in Figure 2.8:

Figure 2.8

276 − ▲ = 286 − ▇

You may wish to ask the children to generate different possible solutions to this problem and record them on a table. This will help them see the relationship between the two numbers chosen and may then help them generalise with particular calculations. Doing this kind of activity with different mathematical operations supports children's reasoning about and therefore understanding of the nature of the different mathematical operations.

Reasoning in support of calculation strategies

Reasoning about different calculations may also support the children to develop efficient calculation strategies, which are founded on a clear understanding of the operation, rather than a half-remembered set of tricks and processes. Your choice of examples will be important here. Consider the example in Figure 2.9:

Figure 2.9

49 + 17 = 50 + ▢

As the children complete calculations like this one, they may then be in a better position to calculate 49 + 17 by realising that it is the same as 50 + 16 (they might conceptualise this as taking one from the 17 and 'giving' it to the 49 to make 50. 50 + 16 is a much easier calculation to do mentally than 49 + 17. An understanding of the logical relations between the numbers and the nature of the addition operation enables the children to carry out this calculation with understanding rather than trying to remember whether to add or subtract one from the 17.

Consider the calculation in Figure 2.10:

Figure 2.10

49 − 17 = 50 − ▢

In doing this calculation, the children may realise that the adding one to the minuend (the first number in the subtraction calculation) means that you have to add one to the subtrahend (the number that is being subtracted) to keep the difference between them the same. As 50 − 18 is a much easier calculation than 49 − 17, spending time reasoning about calculation may lead children to adopt efficient mental calculation strategies.

So far in this chapter, we have considered a number of rich tweaks, to help develop the children's reasoning about calculation.

In the following section, we consider other ways to encourage children to reason with calculation and use multiplication as our example. It should be stressed here that the strategies outlined earlier will work with all operations and the one explored in the following will also work with all operations.

Rich Tweak 5 – Reasoning from a given calculation

Rather than having an unknown in a calculation and inviting the children to reason their way to working out what that unknown is, a further rich tweak is to give children a completed calculation and invite them to come up with other calculations, which are derived by reasoning.

Consider the calculation in Figure 2.11:

Figure 2.11

$49 \times 17 = 833$

It would then be possible for the children to derive other calculations related to the one in Figure 2.12:

Figure 2.12

$50 \times 17 = ?$

The intention here, as with Rich Tweak 1, is that the children do not simply try to calculate the answer to the question but that the calculation is sufficiently challenging that reasoning the answer is a more efficient strategy.

Rich Tweak 5 – case study

Mrs Hulse teaches in Year 1. Her children have a good knowledge of counting up to 100 and are able to identify one more and one less than any number between 0 and 100. Some of them are confident in finding two more and two less. They have also been practising counting forwards and backwards in 2s, 5s and 10s from any number between 0 and 100.

Chloe and the other children in her maths group were confident with these skills and had begun to perform basic addition and subtraction calculations, some of which crossed multiples of 10 (e.g. 4 + 7 = ?; 12 − 5 = ?). Mrs Hulse, being a good teacher, had already incorporated Rich Tweak 1, and Chloe and her friends were able to calculate 7 + ? = 11).

Mrs Hulse then gave Chloe the statement that 27 + 8 = 35. Chloe checked that this was correct by carefully counting on 8 from 27 and getting to 35. Mrs Hulse then presented Chloe with the calculation 27 + 7 = ? and asked her to try to work it out 'without counting'. She asked Chloe to point out anything that was the same about the first calculation (27 + 8 = 35) and the second. Having identified that the 27 was the same, Chloe then went on to reason that the answer must be 34, as 'it is one less than 35 and 7 is one less than 8.'

It should be noted here that the questions used to draw the children into the process of reasoning are important here. If Mrs Hulse had simply presented Chloe and her friends with the two calculations, it is unlikely that they would have been able to engage in the reasoning needed to find the unknown in the second calculation. We feel that teachers should not assume that children will simply 'pick up' how to reason but need to be shown. We are, however, confident that mathematical reasoning is a skill that can be developed through careful teaching.

Nunes et al. (2015) are unequivocal in their assertion that mathematical reasoning can be taught to children in primary schools. They state:

> These results establish that primary school teachers can actively teach mathematical reasoning to children.
> (Nunes et al., 2015, p. 5)

Thinking about your own practice. Whatever year group you teach, think about some calculation work that you are going to be undertaking with your class. Choose a starting calculation (any operation) and then compose five further questions that you might give to the children, which they could work out through a process of reasoning.

Robert Kaplinsky's 'open middle' problems

Robert Kaplinsky has a fantastic resource for encouraging children to engage with calculation in a way that develops reasoning (and number fluency). He terms his problems 'open middle' to reflect the fact that they have the same opening for all children and the same end-point (frequently, there is a best answer), but the way to get to the answer, the 'middle' part of the problem, is much more open. This encourages children to explore and try things out.

What about the problem of something like, having digit cards 1 to 9 and being able to use each one once only, try to make a two-digit plus two-digit calculation that is as close to 100 as possible. This is quite straightforward but can easily be expanded to include calculations like the one shown in Figure 2.13:

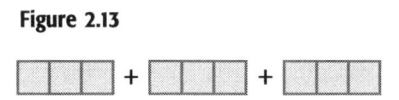

Figure 2.13

☐☐☐ + ☐☐☐ + ☐☐☐

In this situation, the children are given the digit cards 1 to 9 as before and are only allowed to use each card once. The challenge is to come up with the sum that is closest to 1000. Hopefully you can see that this type of question can easily be tweaked to fit the operation you are working on, and to fit the children you are teaching.

Robert Kaplinsky's hugely helpful 'Open Middle' website provides a number of these questions. We include a list of some of our favourites at the end of this chapter. The 'Open Middle' website is available at the following link:

www.openmiddle.com/

Before we leave the idea of Open Middle problems, we would like to prompt you to consider how this kind of exercise could be developed to include calculations with fractions. In his interview with Craig Barton (the *Mr Barton Maths Podcast*), Robert Kaplinsky gives this wonderful example of using digit cards to compare fractions. In the activity, children are given digit cards 1 to 9 and have to arrange them to make a fraction in the form shown in Figure 2.14, which is as close to 1 as possible.

In his online course, Kaplinsky makes the point that there are a significant number of children who would very comfortably complete questions in which they have to compare two fractions and decide which is bigger, but who wouldn't be able to complete the question below.

Given the digit cards 1 to 9 (and using each one no more than once), create a fraction that is as close to 1 as possible:

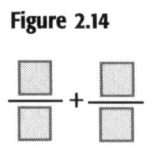

Figure 2.14

$$\frac{\square}{\square} + \frac{\square}{\square}$$

He questions what it is that the children who could do the simple task but would really have to think hard about this challenge. We feel that this kind of challenge suits the kind of children that the National Curriculum document identifies as having grasped a basic concept quickly but who require a further challenge to deepen and enrich their understanding. Again, we want to stress that this kind of question is not a starting point in a sequence of learning; the children need to have had experience of comparing fractions before they tackle this.

Function machines

Another way to encourage your children's ability to reason about number is to make use of function machines. The children will probably be familiar with function machines such as the one shown in Figure 2.15.

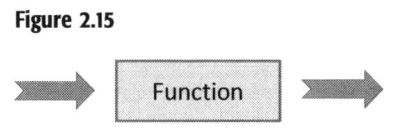

Figure 2.15

These can be fun ways to frame calculations, and they also get away from the purely abstract symbols we find in other calculation questions. To move away from simply using abstract calculations, Mrs Steward was working with her Year 3 class using function machines. She first presented the children with the function machine shown in Figure 2.16.

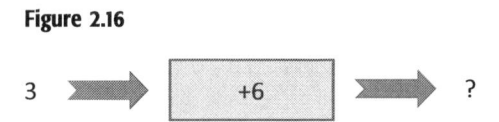

Figure 2.16

After a little practice with these she then gave them the example in Figure 2.17:

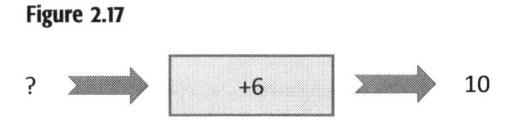

Figure 2.17

Crucial to her teaching, in every example, Mrs Steward asked the children to discuss what they thought the answer might be and to give their reasons. In both of the examples above the 'function' of the machine was known but the problems presented are different. Add 6 to 3 is a different proposition than being asked, 'What do I need to have started with so that adding 6 will produce 9?' As you may note this use of function machines is very similar to the missing-number problems we saw earlier. However, the addition of these machines can sometimes help children to contextualise the activity a little more.

Moving on, Mrs Steward then asked the children to consider the example in Figure 2.18:

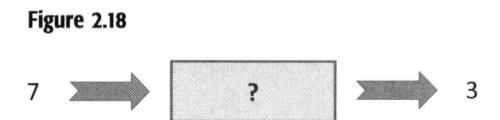

Figure 2.18

7 ⟹ [?] ⟹ 3

Here the children were asked to consider what 'function' is been applied to give the answer. The children must use their knowledge of both mathematical operations and number to reason the answer. Once again discussion amongst the children is key here to helping them develop their reasoning and mathematical explanation skills. The role of talk here cannot be underestimated. Much has been written about the importance of asking children to explain their reasoning as a method of not only sharing their understanding but also embedding knowledge (for a fuller discussion, see Littleton and Mercer, 2013).

Next the real fun begins, crafty Mrs Steward offer the children the function machine shown in Figure 2.19.

Figure 2.19

5 ⟹ [?] ⟹ 10

At first all seem straight forward but the children became a little confused when Mrs Steward refused to accept +5 as an answer. She explained that while that would have worked that is not the function of this particular machine. Still confused, Mrs Steward offered them a chance to put another number into the machine. Wayne suggested putting 4 into the machine and out came 8, Fatima suggested 9 and out came 18. After some further discussion, many of the children realised that the machine doubles, and some even suggested that the function was ×2. This introduced the idea to the children that perhaps just one number passing through the machine was not enough to be sure of what it does.

All this, however, is in preparation for what she really wanted to do with the children. The following day Mrs Steward gave the children the function machine shown in Figure 2.20.

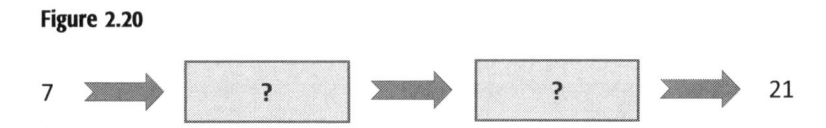

Figure 2.20

7 ⇒ [?] ⇒ [?] ⇒ 21

A few pairs of children suggested possible solutions, but, as Mrs Steward pointed out, they can't both be right. Fatima remembered back to the day before and asked if they could put in some more numbers.

This input–output analysis allowed the children to really start to reason and share their thinking with each other about calculation as well as encouraged them to do multiple mental calculations at the same time.

Chapter summary

In this chapter we have considered a number of 'rich tweaks', which we hope will enable you to offer opportunities for mathematical thinking to your children in the context of calculation. As we stated at the beginning, we are clear that these tweaks are not a replacement for clear and focused teaching about calculation and should not be used with children until they have an understanding of calculation. However, once this is established, these tweaks will allow them to explore and develop their understanding in several different ways.

Rich Tweaks – Calculation	
Standard Activity	**Rich Tweak Activity**
Complete calculations in a standard format.	Vary the position of the unknown
Comparing two fractions	Using four of the digits between 1 and 9 (and not using the same one twice), create a fraction in the form of a double-digit number (numerator) over a double-digit number (denominator) which is as close to 1 as possible.
Add two double-digit numbers using the standard vertical algorithm	Using the digit cards 1 to 9 (and not using any digit twice), create a subtraction calculation of two double-digit numbers (i.e. a double-digit number – a double-digit number) which has an answer as close to 49 as possible. We recommend several variations to this, that is varying the 'target' number.
Add three three-digit numbers using the standard vertical algorithm	Using all your 1–9 digit cards (but not using any digit more than once), create three three-digit numbers with a sum as close to 1000 as possible.
Complete calculations in a standard format	Use function machines to explore the effects of changing particular inputs, to explore which inputs must have led to a given output, or to explore what the function machine does to the input number

References

Christodoulou, D. (2017) *Seven Myths in Education*. Oxford: Oxford University Press.

Department for Education (2014) *The National Curriculum in England: Complete Framework for Key Stages* 1 to 4. Available from: https://www.gov.uk/government/publications/national-curriculum-in-england-framework-for-key-stages-1-to-4 (Accessed: 15th of September 2021).

Gilmore, C., Clayton, S., Cragg, L., McKeaveney, C., Simms, V. and Johnson, S. (2018) Understanding arithmetic concepts: The role of domain-specific and domain-general skills. *PLoS One*, 13(9), pp. 1–20.

Haylock, D. (2014) *Mathematics Explained for Primary Teachers* (5th Edition). London: Sage.

Kaplinsky, R. *Open Middle Problems*. Available from: www.openmiddle.com/.

Littleton, K. and Mercer, N. (2013) *Interthinking: Putting Talk to Work*. London: Routledge.

Nunes, T., Bryant, P., Evans, D., Bell, D., Gardner, S., Gardner, A. and Carraher, J. (2009) The contribution of logical reasoning to the learning of mathematics in primary school. *British Journal of Developmental Psychology*, 25(1), pp. 147–166.

Nunes, T., Bryant, P., Evans, D., Gottardis, L. and Terlektsi, M.E. (2015) *Teaching Mathematical Reasoning: Probability and Problem Solving in Primary School*. London: Nuffield Foundation.

Skemp, R. (1976) Relational understanding and instrumental understanding. *Mathematics Teaching*, 77(1), pp. 20–26.

3
Reasoning in geometry and statistics

Chapter overview

In this chapter, we explore the possibilities for applying 'rich tweaks' to activities about geometry and statistics. We invite you into think about three teaching episodes, where the teachers involved have all made use of rich tweaks to offer the children opportunities for mathematical reasoning. The first case study takes us into Mrs Strummer's classroom, where she is using skilful questioning to adapt a standard 'hidden shapes' activity to create opportunities for reasoning. This is contrasted with Mr Wilson in the parallel class, who is using the same activity but in a less sophisticated way.

The second example follows a group of children as they discuss a graph showing a day in the life of a pet. In this scenario, the teacher again chooses her questions carefully to ensure that a rich discussion, full of mathematical reasoning, takes place. In the final example, we meet 'Tess' as she grapples with some questions about area and perimeter. We examine how a teacher might tweak activities to encourage reasoning and how a very thorough understanding of an activity can allow a teacher to support children as they find their own points of interest and exploration. The chapter ends with a number of activity suggestions with some 'rich tweaks' that you can adapt and explore with your own children.

Introduction

There is a debate about whether reasoning is a domain-general skill, which can be developed in one context and then applied in different contexts. The research evidence (see Christodoulou, 2017, Chapter 5, for an interesting summary; see also Willingham, 2009) suggests that this is not really the case; being able to reason about mathematics does not mean that the same child will be able to reason about history. The same thinking (that good reasoning is heavily dependent on context-specific knowledge) suggests that reasoning skills do not readily transfer across different areas of mathematics (Willingham makes the point that a child who can reason about the causes of the American Civil War may not also be able to reason about the causes of the First World War). So, the reasoning about number that we considered in Chapter 2 may well not transfer to reasoning about geometry and statistics, which are the areas to which we now turn.

Activities which require logical thinking provide excellent opportunities to develop reasoning skills, and therefore, in the case studies presented in this chapter, much of the reasoning lies in the systematic building of chains of logical statements or where information needs to be evaluated. The husband and wife Van Hiele team have conducted extensive research into the development of children's reasoning about geometry (see Way, 2011, for an interesting summary). They suggest that children pass through various stages in their understanding of shapes from visualisation (recognition) to analysis (being able to discuss properties of shapes using correct vocabulary) to informal deduction, which Haylock (2014) characterises as

> [c]hildren are able to recognize relationships between and among properties of shapes or classes of shapes and are able to follow logical arguments using these properties.
>
> (p. 393)

The 'shape reveal game' and the 'reasoning about area and perimeter' case studies both have a variety of possible starting points again requiring children to think or work logically and systematically to reason about which possibilities fit with the presented scenario and which do not. However, throughout all the case studies presented in this chapter, the teacher's role is vital. This is apparent (and exemplified in the following) through good role modelling, talk and teacher questioning. As with all the examples presented in this book, the following case studies are activities which have originated from everyday classroom activities but have been tweaked in simple ways to enhance the reasoning opportunities open to the children.

Case Study 3.1 – Reasoning about the properties of shapes; 'Guess the Shape'.

Original Activity – Name the shape being revealed

It should be made clear from the outset that this activity is not intended to teach children basic information about the properties of shapes. Children need to be taught that information explicitly and doing so is highly important; those facts about the properties of shapes are what enable the children to engage in geometric reasoning. The following activity assumes some knowledge of the property of shapes and is designed primarily to develop reasoning in that context.

The shape-reveal task is one that is commonly used in primary schools. Our experience is that is it often used more as a 'guess the shape' activity. Let's go into Mr Wilson's classroom . . .

Figure 3.1

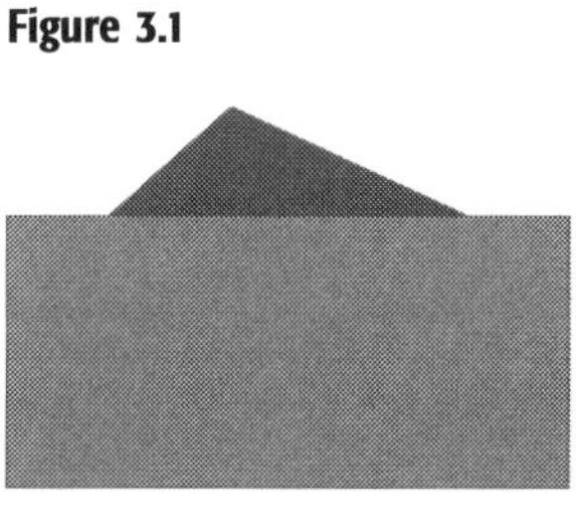

Mr Wilson has spent time teaching the children about the properties of some simple two-dimensional (2D) shapes. He has displayed the image above on the whiteboard and asked them to think about what the (hidden) shape could be. Several children take a guess, and one of them, Connor, has guessed correctly. However, Mr Wilson has decided not to stop the activity immediately and is allowing several children to express their thoughts. He is keen that as many children as possible give an answer and that there is a range of possible opinions in the room. He asks Connor and a couple of the other children to explain why they thought the hidden shape was a triangle, a pentagon and so on. The game continues, with more of the shape being revealed and the children revising their guesses.

There is limited scope for reasoning in this scenario. Zoe suggests that the hidden shape is a triangle. Mr Wilson asks a follow-up question: 'What makes you think it is a triangle?' Zoe is unsure and responds that the shape looks like a triangle. She thinks a little longer and says that it must have three sides because two are visible and there must be another one to join them together. While Zoe is clearly engaging her understanding of the properties of a triangle, the scope for reasoning is very limited.

There is more scope to develop reasoning if a child makes a guess that is clearly wrong. The following dialogue develops:

> Bruce – I think it's a square.
> Mr Wilson – Why do you think it's a square, Bruce? (By not simply dismissing Bruce's suggestion as incorrect, Mr Wilson is allowing Bruce to engage in more mathematical reasoning).
> Bruce – You can see one of the corners, but the other three are hidden.
> Stevie – I don't think it can be a square. That corner we can see doesn't have a right angle, and square only have right angles.

This is precisely the kind of reasoning that this activity is designed to elicit, but it has only emerged by chance. With that thought in mind, this activity can be tweaked easily to encourage deeper reasoning. We feel that by far the best question to being this activity with is the following:

Rich Tweak 3.1 – What shape could this not be and why?

In the parallel classroom, Mrs Strummer is also teaching this activity. She has decided on a different question than simply asking the children to guess the shape. Her question is

'Which shape is it definitely not, and how do you know?'

By explaining what the shape cannot be, the children immediately have to engage their understanding, and Mrs Strummer is not reliant on an incorrect, or impossible, guess for the reasoning to occur. She offers the children a scaffolded reasoning sentence which helps them give fuller reasons in this activity and sends a message to all the children about the quality of the reasoning that she expects.

'The shape cannot be a _____ because _____ and _____.'

Clarence is excited by this question and immediately says, 'It cannot be a circle'. While this is correct, the reasoning that the child has engaged in is not necessarily visible to the rest of the class. Mrs Strummer is keen to acknowledge Clarence's enthusiasm but also wants her to answer more fully so that her reasoning is made visible to the rest of the children. Using the earlier sentence structure, Mrs Strummer asks Clarence for more information:

Clarence – It can't be a circle.
Mrs Strummer – You're right, Clarence. Can you explain how you know, using our sentence?
Clarence – It can't be a circle because it has a corner.
Mrs Strummer – That's great, Clarence. Excellent reasoning. Can you finish off the sentence?
Clarence is a little unsure, but Jake offers to help
Jake – It can't be a circle because it has a corner, and circles have no corners.
Well done, Jake and Clarence. Let's say that sentence all together.

Reasoning in geometry and statistics ◆ 45

While the reasoning involved in the final part of the sentence might be obvious to some of the children in the class, it will not necessarily be so to others, so insisting that the sentence is said in full will really help those children.

It is possible that the children in your class may never have been asked a 'What is it not?' kind of question before and may not immediately respond. It is always good to have a range of questions ready in case the first one does not get the response you require. In this case, you might want to prompt the children by asking, 'Is it a circle?' (many children will be quite clear that the hidden shape is not a circle), then 'How do you know it isn't a circle?' The likely response to this is something akin to the second part of the scaffolded sentence suggested earlier. You may then need to encourage or model the final part of the sentence. Patti has a different reason for it not being a circle:

> Patti – The hidden shape can't be a circle because it has straight sides.
> Mrs – Strummer: And . . .
> Patti – And a circle has no straight sides.
> Mrs – Strummer: Excellent. Let's say that sentence all together.

Once this form of words has been rehearsed a couple of times, the children are likely to use it with less and less prompting.

Mrs Strummer has thought carefully about the shape, and the part of it that she has chosen to reveal. This is important. The activity works best and elicits more reasoning if there are several relatively obvious shapes that can be eliminated easily. In the example shown earlier, it is clear that the angle shown is bigger than a right angle. This is very deliberate as this supports the children to see that the hidden shape cannot be a square, oblong, equilateral triangle, and so on. It should be clear at this point that successful reasoning about why the hidden shape cannot be an equilateral triangle (for example) requires quite a lot of prior knowledge about the properties of an equilateral triangle, which the children will not learn through this activity. In addition to giving careful thought to what the hidden shape is and how much of it is revealed initially, it will also be worthwhile spending some time considering which shapes can be discounted before more of the shape is revealed. It is possible that none of the children in your class will mention that the shape cannot be an equilateral triangle. If nobody does, it would be worth asking the class whether the hidden shape can be an equilateral triangle.

Once there has been considerable discussion and reasoning about what the shape cannot be and the children have become used to responding using the suggested form of words, Mrs Strummer moves the activity on, by revealing more of the hidden shape (see Figure 3.2).

Figure 3.2

She has planned carefully; revealing more of the shape enables the children to discount more shapes. This should now allow them to eliminate any kind of triangle. Max is looking quizzically at the shape and asks whether the two sides will ever meet. Mrs Strummer asks if anyone knows the particular mathematical word that is used to describe lines, or sides of a shape, that never meet. Garry says that the word is *parallel*, and many of the class agree. Max is now able to explain his own reasoning in more detail.

Max – The hidden shape can't be a triangle because I can see three sides, but two of them will never meet. This means there must be more than three sides.

Mrs Strummer – Can you remember the special word for sides, or lines, that never meet?

Max – Oh, yes. *Parallel*. So, it can't be a triangle, because I can see three sides, but two of them are parallel, so there must be another side.

At this point, most of the children became quite convinced that the hidden shape is a parallelogram. In order to push their thinking a little further, Mrs Strummer asks a further question.

Mrs Strummer – So, a lot of you seem convinced that the shape is a parallelogram. Could it be anything else, like a pentagon, or a hexagon, or even an octagon?

This acts as a useful diagnostic question; Danny is adamant that it cannot be a hexagon; he may be unable to visualise hexagons that are not prototypical regular hexagons. If there are children who are clear that it cannot be a hexagon or a pentagon, this might be a signal that they need to be exposed to a range of irregular polygons.

After the mathematically rich discussion described earlier, Mrs Strummer gives the children the task to develop their own 'Hidden Shape' activities, getting them to note down which shapes can be discounted from the first reveal of the shape and which additional ones can be discounted following a further reveal. This requires more sophisticated reasoning and will require them to draw on their understanding of the properties of shape. Some of the children may well wish to try to fool their classmates (see Figure 3.3).

Figure 3.3

We really like shape reveal activities as a way to get children to reason about the properties of shapes. This kind of activity can be used with any group of children who have an understanding of the properties of simple shapes; so, you could use it with Year 2 children or Year 6 children. You would choose different shapes and what you reveal. Here are some key statements and questions that you might use with this activity.

Key Questions/Statements:

This shape cannot be a . . . because it has/does not have . . .
What makes you think that this is NOT a . . .
What shape could this NOT be?
How do you know that this is not a . . . ?
Could this shape be any type of triangle/quadrilateral? Why/why not?

Case Study 3.2 – Reasoning about statistics: 'A day in the life of a pet dog'.

Original Activity – Display the data in a graph
Rich Tweak – What does the data in this graph tell us? How do you know?

In many primary classrooms, statistics activities involve the collection and display of data. Children undertake surveys of favourite foods or colours and so on and then display the data in a chart. However, such activities are often time-consuming and offer little opportunities for reasoning to occur. It is within the analysis and interpretation of data that the really rich opportunities for reasoning lie. Children still need to be taught how to gather and display data, but the balance between this and time spent on analysis and interpretation should be carefully considered. The rich tweak described here therefore presents the children with the data and asks them to interpret what it shows supported by structured and varied questions asked by the teacher. In interpreting and reasoning about the data displayed, children engage with a deep understanding of the nature of how the graph is used to convey information.

During this activity a group of children, Dylan, Curtis, Lewis and Mya were given a copy of Figure 3.4 showing the heart rate of a pet dog over a day.

Figure 3.4

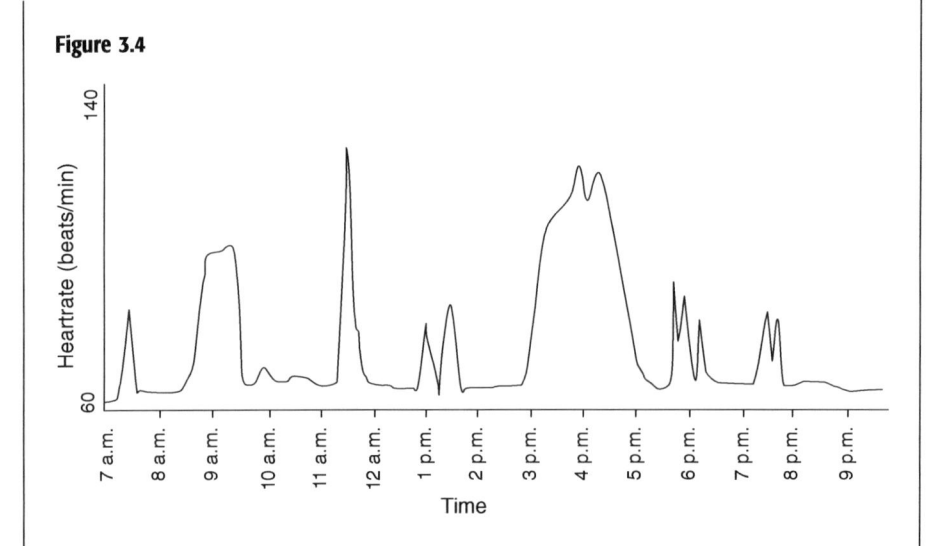

To begin with, the teacher simply asked the children what they noticed and what this could show. This initial question enabled the children to describe what they saw, such as the labels on the axis and what the changes in the line could mean. They began to speculate what each of the peaks might relate to and connected these to periods of activity for the dog. Open-ended questions such as 'What do you notice?' enable all children to participate at an accessible level and can therefore encourage them to suggest hypotheses and to make connections with the data and the real-life scenario presented. Barton (2018) calls these 'goal-free problems', that is questions or problems in which the children are not asked to find a particular answer but are given the freedom to look at information and identify what they can from it.

A similarly useful open-ended question is, 'Can you spot any patterns?' When the group were asked this, Dylan noticed that some of the peaks were 'wide and flat' and some of them were 'sharp and pointy'. At this point, the teacher asked the group if they could explain why this might be, expressly inviting them to speculate and reason. Lewis suggested that the sharp point could have been when the dog's heart rate rose as he was excited about something for a short length of time, such as a visitor at the door or something similar. To encourage the group to engage in more explorative talk, the teacher then opened this up further by asking Curtis if he could build on what Lewis had said, helping the children to build logical chains of statements. Curtis suggested that the wider peaks were showing when the dog's heart rate was raised for a longer period but that the dog was not as excited as before, justifying this with reference to the line of the graph and suggesting that this perhaps showed when the dog went for a walk. None of the children had mentioned the smaller peaks between 3 and 4 p.m., so the teacher directed attention towards these by saying, 'I notice that here are some small peaks here. Can you explain why?' After some discussion the children decided that it was because someone was throwing a ball for the dog whilst on the walk.

To assess more specific understanding further, the teacher in this case study asked questions adapted from a stem of

'Can you give an example of . . . ?'
For example: 'Can you give an example of when the dog was resting?'
Can you give an example of when the heart rate was slowing down?'

Rather than simply accepting an answer, following this up with a secondary question such as 'Are you sure?' 'Why do you think that?' or 'How do you know that?' encourages children to explain and justify their thinking. Not only does this provide excellent assessment information for the teacher, but it also shares understanding with the rest of the group.

Once the teacher was confident about the level of understanding, she began to ask the children questions which would require them to reason more deeply and draw inferences from their manipulation of the data. To do this teachers can ask questions using a stem such as 'What if . . . ?'.

Here are some examples:

'What would happen to the line if the bottom axis was extended to be 24 hours?
'What would happen if the dog started chasing a bird during its morning walk?'
'What would happen if the owner had forgotten to feed the dog at lunchtime?'

'What would happen if a visitor came to the house at 8 p.m.?'
'What would it mean if this line was not as steep?

When the teacher asked what would the graph look like if the dog had not gone out for a walk in the morning the group agreed that the line would remain flat at the resting heart rate level between 8 and 10 a.m. However, Curtis then remarked that the dog would probably not be so tired for the rest of the day and would be more active for the rest of the afternoon. He then sketched out a graph showing lots of smaller peaks during the afternoon period which he stated showed the dog playing at home. This activity offered the teacher rich assessment information showing that the group truly understood what they were being shown and that they had connected their reasoning to the reality of the scenario presented and used this to infer further possibilities. Questions that use a 'What would happen if...' stem often provide these rich opportunities.

The context used in this activity was important. Using a scenario which was familiar to the children meant that the teacher was able to use a variety of open-ended questions to encourage reasoning. Questions such as 'What is it about the line graph that tells us that the dog likes his food?' 'Why doesn't the line in the graph go all the way down to 0?" 'Why does the peak flatten off and not continue to rise when the dog is walking?' were used throughout the session.

Understanding the context enabled the children to engage with and understand the data demonstrated in the graph at an accessible level. They knew about the things that dogs do and so could use this wider knowledge to interpret the graph. The context encouraged them to engage in the discussions and motivated them to take part. However, understanding could be so closely related to the context that the activity may need to be built on through another context to ensure that the comprehension gained in this activity could be transferred. During a follow-up session, the children created their own 'story graphs' and asked each other questions about them using question stems provided by the teacher.

Key Questions/Statements:

Why does the graph/line . . . ?
What do you notice?
Can you point to an example of . . . ?
Can you spot any patterns?
Can you explain why we see . . . here?
What would happen if . . . ?
What is it about the graph that tells us that . . . ?
Why doesn't the graph/line . . . ?

Case Study 3.3 – Reasoning about area and perimeter – drawing rectangles

Original Activity – Calculate the area/ perimeter of the shape
Rich Tweak – Draw a shape with a perimeter of . . . / an area of . . .

The following example is about geometry and is intended to demonstrate how engagement with a rich problem can lead to further questions and problems, often coming from the children involved in the problem. Here is an example of a child (Tess) working through this problem (Figure 3.5).

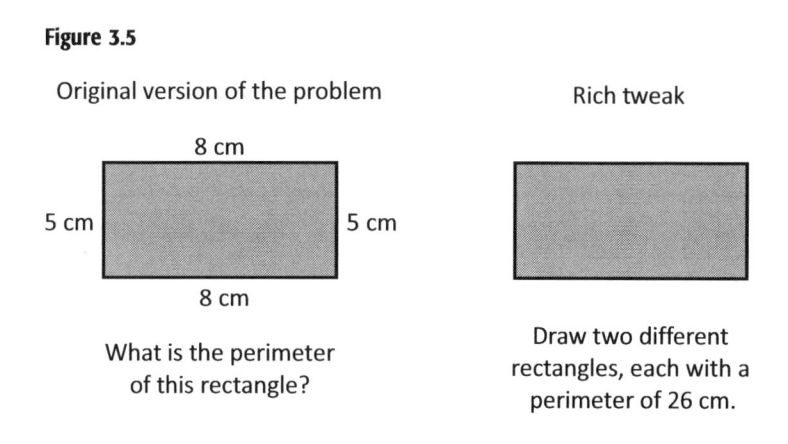

Figure 3.5

Original version of the problem

8 cm
5 cm   5 cm
8 cm

What is the perimeter of this rectangle?

Rich tweak

Draw two different rectangles, each with a perimeter of 26 cm.

The original question (What is the perimeter of this shape?) can be answered by simply adding together all the given numbers without any real understanding of perimeter. Tess was presented with a rich tweak version of this (can you draw two different rectangles with a perimeter of 26 cm), which takes no more time to plan. This version cannot be answered without an understanding of perimeter and offers children more choice and agency about their work. There are many correct answers, and this fact alone might lead children to persist once they have found two examples (see Figure 3.6).

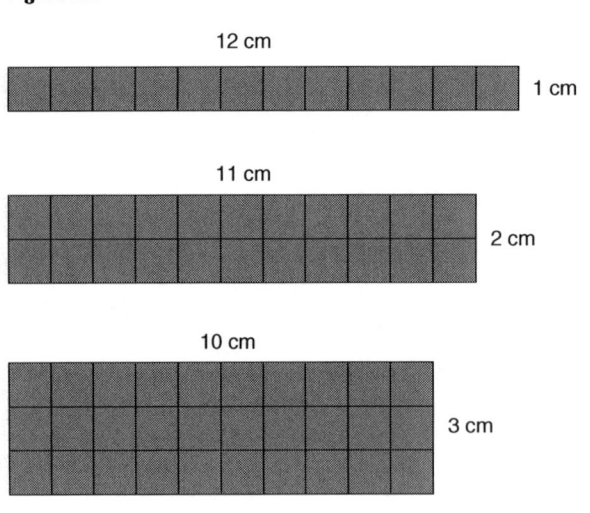

Figure 3.6

12 cm
1 cm

11 cm
2 cm

10 cm
3 cm

Having a good understanding of the problem enabled the teacher to know that systematic recording could lead to prompting Tess to think more deeply about the problem. With some prompting, Tess began to record her answers in a systematic way, and having done so, it became clear that there were more than two rectangles with a perimeter of 26 cm. The teacher then prompted Tess to think about how many rectangles with this perimeter there could be. The teacher also had a range of additional questions and strategies to move the child's thinking to a deeper level. Asking Tess to record her thinking on squared paper led her to think about the areas of the rectangles that had been created. Doing so, it became clear that the rectangles were not 'all the same size'; that is, they had different areas. For many children, the discovery that rectangles with the same perimeter do not have the same area is significant.

As a result of this new discovery, Tess then began to explore the areas of rectangles, looking at how many different rectangles she could make with a given area, in this case 24 cm². You might want to do that now before you read on.

Initially, Tess played with the idea, drawing rectangles and calculating the area. There was some evidence of trial and error at work until she realised that she was sometimes drawing the same rectangle in a different orientation. Looking at some of the lengths she had written she stated that it reminded her of some of the times tables questions that she knew, and she therefore she started to draw on her multiplication understanding. At this stage, the teacher decided to play 'devil's advocate' and stated that she thought there must be 12 different rectangles with an area of 24 cm². Giving a 'hypothesis' like this encourages the child to prove or disprove what has been suggested. Initially, Tess agreed, stating that there could not be 24 as 'you would draw the same rectangle twice, just the other way round'. She then began to work systematically to prove her (and the teacher's) hypothesis.

She began by drawing the following rectangles 1 × 24, 2 × 12, 3 × 8, 4 × 6, reaching a rectangle of 5 × . . . was a sticking point. Using wider knowledge she realised that 24 was not divisible by 5. This then led her to re-evaluate her earlier hypothesis that there would be 12 rectangles and to conclude that there were only 4 ('because there are 8 factors of 24 and therefore only 4 rectangles').

At this point, Tess wondered if she could solve the problem by drawing a square. Sometimes, children will make unexpected suggestions, which the teacher has not anticipated. At these points, you may have to make a decision about the direction in which you want the learning to proceed. In this instance, this could have led to a discussion about the possibility of using decimal measurements. In fact, the teacher used this as an opportunity for an (interesting) discussion about the differences and similarities between a square and a rectangle. Tess looked back at her workings and realised that this could not be done as the nearest square would be 5 × 5, prompting a realisation that square numbers make a square shape. Ensuring that you as a teacher are as familiar as possible with activities before setting them enables you to devise prompts such as this for yourself in case such points are not noticed by the children.

Having explored this one avenue, the problem drew to a close. A feature of rich problems is that there are natural stopping points, but there are always possibilities for further learning; there will be other avenues to explore. This involves being prepared to relinquish some control and to embrace some of the wider learning and problem-solving. Being well prepared for these tasks involves knowing where the mathematics might lead, where you want it to go (and therefore having questions ready to steer it back on course if necessary).

Key Questions/Statements:

What is the same and what is different about . . . ?
I think that there might be . . .
Will it always be the case that . . . ?
Could you solve it by drawing a . . . ?

Summary

Once you have tried a few examples of turning everyday questions into rich mathematical tasks it becomes relatively easy to spot opportunities to do this. But the success of a rich task goes beyond simply making it available to children. For learning within rich tasks to really thrive there needs to be a classroom ethos whereby children can discuss their ideas and understanding with confidence that they will be welcomed and considered. Rich tasks and good questioning thrive in an atmosphere in which children are happy to give ideas without fear of being wrong or shamed. The emphasis should be on methods rather than answers and there should be a classroom ethos whereby mistakes and misconceptions are welcomed and used as learning points.

Key questions

>What makes you think that this is a . . . (circle, parallelogram etc)?
>Which shape could this not possibly be?
>What do you notice about . . . ?
>Can you give me an example of . . . ?
>Can you build on what . . . has said?
>What is it (about the graph) that shows you that . . . ?
>I notice that . . . Can you explain why?
>What would happen if I changed . . . ?
>Alternatively . . .
>Pose an incorrect hypothesis
>Make an incorrect suggestion
>Point out something that you notice that the children do not

Rich Tweaks – Angles	
Standard Activity	**Rich Tweak Activity**
Measure the angles in a shape	True or false – a shape that has more than 4 sides only has obtuse angles True or false – the angles in a triangle are always acute

Rich Tweaks – Statistics	
Standard Activity	**Rich Tweak Activity**
Collecting data/drawing graphs and charts	Show different representations of the same data, e.g. standard graphs, infographics, box and whisker graphs. Which works best for, e.g. showing upper and lower extremes, means and medians, enables easiest comparisons to be made, best illustrates main points, shows trends, makes data accessible and understandable.

Rich Tweaks – Tessellation/capacity	
Standard Activity	**Rich Tweak Activity**
Explore which shapes tesselate in 2D and 3D	You need to make a drinks container out of 2D shapes. Which shape would be the best to use so that you don't waste too much material? Which 3D is the best for packing lots of drinks containers into a box?

Rich Tweaks – Properties of shapes	
Standard Activity	**Rich Tweak Activity**
Show shapes and discuss properties	If all people were shapes, which shape would you be and why?

Rich Tweaks – Properties of shapes	
Standard Activity	**Rich Tweak Activity**
Draw/identify a shape	Which is the odd one out? Why?

Rich Tweaks – Properties of shapes	
Standard Activity	**Rich Tweak Activity**
Draw/identify a shape	What is the same about these shapes? What is different about them?

Rich Tweaks – Properties of Shapes	
Standard Activity	**Rich Tweak Activity**
Describe/list the properties of a shape.	Without you partner seeing, draw a shape on a sticky note and stick it onto your partner's forehead. Your partner must ask you questions about the properties of the shapes that you have drawn to guess which shape they are.

Rich Tweaks – Properties of Shapes	
Standard Activity	**Rich Tweak Activity**
Describe/list the properties of a shape.	Draw a shape in each corner or the room/playground (or on a piece of paper). Ask the children to identify which shape(s) matches the statement read out by running to the correct corner or pointing to the correct shape. For example A shape with a right angle A shape with a right angle and only 3 sides A shape where all the angles are equal A shape where all the angles are equal and add up to 180 A quadrilateral with equal sides A quadrilateral with equal sides but no right angles. Once the children have made their selection ask them to explain why they have selected their answer and dismissed the other answers.

Rich Tweaks – Properties of Shapes	
Standard Activity	**Rich Tweak Activity**
Draw/identify a triangle	Is this shape still a triangle? How do you know?

Rich Tweaks – Regular and Irregular Shapes	
Standard Activity	**Rich Tweak Activity**
Identify regular/irregular shapes	In groups use string to construct regular irregular versions of the same shape. How do you know that you have made an irregular/regular shape?

Rich Tweaks – Time	
Standard Activity	**Rich Tweak Activity**
	Orla has put these three times in order from shortest to longest. Is she right? 1 month, 1 day, 1 week, 3 weeks, 7 days, 24 hours, 40 days

Rich Tweaks – Measures (weight)	
Standard Activity	**Rich Tweak Activity**
Convert 4,600 g into kg	Khalid has 4½ kg of flour. Jem has 4600 g. Who has more? How do you know?

Rich Tweaks – Perimeter	
Standard Activity	**Rich Tweak Activity**
Measure the perimeter of a shape	Remi has a shape that has a perimeter of 24 cm. Can you draw Remi's shape? Can you draw another shape that Remi's shape could be? How many different shapes can you make?

Rich Tweaks – Perimeter	
Standard Activity	**Rich Tweak Activity**
Measure the perimeter of a shape	Make a shape out of blocks and measure the perimeter. Can you make a shape with a different perimeter using the same blocks and the same number of blocks?

Rich Tweaks – Area	
Standard Activity	**Rich Tweak Activity**
Measure the area of a shape	The area of a shape will be the same as its perimeter. Is this always true, sometimes true, never true?

Rich Tweaks – Properties of shapes	
Standard Activity	**Rich Tweak Activity**
Listing properties of a shape or matching properties to a shape	Can you cut this shape up to make one square and two different sized rectangles?

	Draw a rectangle onto a piece of paper and cut it out. Now cut up your rectangle into 4 or 5 smaller rectangles. Rearrange these smaller rectangles to make a new shape. Does this new shape have the same area as the original rectangle?
Describe the properties of these shapes	Which shape would you choose to: build a house with, play sports with, eat your food with, make a toy out of and so on, and why?

References

Barton, C. (2018) *How I Wish I'd Taught Maths*. Woodbridge: John Catt Educational.

Christodoulou, D. (2017) *Seven Myths in Education*. Oxford: Oxford University Press.

Haylock, D. (2014) *Mathematics Explained for Primary Teachers* (5th Edition). London: Sage.

Way, J. (2011) The development of spatial and geometric thinking: The importance of instruction. *Nrich*. Available from: https://nrich.maths.org/2487 (Accessed: 19 August 2020).

Willingham, D. (2009) *Why Don't Students Like School?* San Francisco: Wiley-Blackwell.

4
Problem-solving

Introduction

The joy of mathematical problem-solving is that it can be used in any aspect of maths and at any stage of learning. However, as it can be so pervasive throughout the curriculum, it is important that it is done well. In this chapter, we consider what is meant by mathematical problem-solving, the skills and strategies involved in solving mathematical problems and ways that teachers can ensure that all children experience-rich mathematical opportunities.

Mathematical problems take many forms, including going beyond simple word problems. Real-life (or pseudo-real-life) problems can provide an engaging context to hook children in and to help them relate maths to their everyday experiences or provide opportunities to apply their understanding and skills. However, sometimes the problem can simply be within maths itself, engendering curiosity about numbers and beyond.

Within maths	To give a difference of 13 what would you take away from 28?
Pseudo–real life/real life	You are a football manager with a budget of £1000K. You need to buy defenders costing £40K each and strikers costing £100K each. If you spend all your money, how many of each could you buy?
Active real-life contexts	If I add up the cost of all the ingredients, what price do I need to sell each cake at the cake sale in order to make a profit?

DOI: 10.4324/9780367808860-5

Mathematical problems offer us the opportunity to develop wider and deeper mathematical reasoning, giving children increased opportunities to choose which strategy or approach to adopt (and to reason and generalise). It is argued that when children are required to identify what maths needs to be done in order to solve the problem (referred to in this chapter as 'seeing the maths') their understanding and sense of number is deepened and their fluency increased (Ofsted, 2011, p. 20, Successful Schools). In fact, Ofsted (2015) reports that

the degree of emphasis on problem solving and conceptual understanding is a key discriminator between good and weaker provision. Where it is under used many pupils spend too long working on straightforward questions, with problem solving located at the ends of exercises or set as extension tasks so that not all tackle them.

Accordingly, the new curriculum is clear about the importance of problem-solving in mathematics, requiring that children

can solve problems by applying their mathematics to a variety of routine and non-routine problems with increasing sophistication, including breaking down problems into a series of simpler steps and persevering in seeking solutions.

Jo Boaler (2015) argues that it is through such activities that children experience the true nature of maths. Imagine a musician only ever learning scales or a footballer only practising penalties. The true nature of music is enjoyed when we play a piece with a band, the skill of the footballer is revealed when working in conjunction with teammates in open, creative play. Boaler argues that often, children's experience of maths is reflective of this repetitive practice-and-drill approach and that when they engage with problem-solving that they explore, experience and have a more fluent, creative experience in which they are able to express themselves and reason mathematically.

Seeing the maths and doing the maths

Many children who may seem otherwise quite competent in maths and can calculate with relative ease can struggle when it comes to mathematical problem-solving. For these children, the issue can be with the transfer of their mathematical understanding to a problem-solving scenario. For example, when children attempt to solve a straightforward calculation, such as 17 + 8 = ?, the method or strategy needed to do this is immediately apparent, the mathematical operation being indicated by the symbol. However, when solving mathematical problems, this may not be quite so obvious. In these activities, children must translate the scenario into numbers and operations for themselves. So if faced with the problem

17 people are in a cafe then 8 more enter, how many are there now?

they would have to translate it into the mathematical equation, 17 + 8 = ? This is an entirely different skill than simply adding 17 to 8. Connecting maths that has been learnt in an abstract format (e.g. straightforward numerical calculations) to a problem-solving scenario in a meaningful way can be difficult, meaning that children who are otherwise capable mathematicians and struggle when it comes to problem-solving.

Mathematical problem-solving therefore involves two elements:

1 An ability to 'see' the maths which needs to be done (i.e. translating the problem into numbers and operations, knowing which operations to apply and how the numbers fit into these)
2 An ability to 'do' the maths contained within the problem (i.e. carrying out the mathematical operations)

Whilst children may be able to 'do' the maths contained within the problem presented to them, some can struggle to 'see' the maths that needs to be done leading to issues when working with mathematical problems.

For some, this may be to do with understanding the language of maths, which can present difficulties. Everyday words such as *point* or *difference* may be used in an unfamiliar manner, carrying a new meaning or entirely new vocabulary may be presented. In fact, Steve Higgins (2003) in the excellent 'Parlez-vous Mathematics?' uses the analogy that the language of mathematics is like learning a foreign language. This can make it difficult for children to translate the scenario presented in the problem into a mathematical form that they can understand.

Rather than giving children overly simplified, formulaic approaches, we need to teach them how to use and apply a range of strategies. Teachers should not assume that children will know these strategies or how to use them, and so each must be taught explicitly alongside examples of how and when they can be applied. This could include encouraging them to look for patterns, making and testing generalisations or working systematically to find all possibilities (all of which are covered in Chapter 5) or sometimes simple trial and improvement.

In this chapter, we look at ways in which teachers can help children with the translating of mathematical problems and develop a range of problem-solving approaches as well as a consideration of the rich tweaks that teachers can employ to enhance these mathematical experiences.

Case Study Activity 1 – Fermi questions

Original Activity – Solving word problems
Rich Tweak – Setting problems requiring children to come up with a method or strategy rather than an answer.

Mr Wiggins had noticed that if he told his mixed Year 4 class which mathematical operation to use the children could solve mathematical problems relatively easily (i.e. they were able to 'do' the maths). However, when they were presented with problems in which they had to deduce possible solution strategies for themselves, they struggled to 'see the maths' required to find a solution. To address this, Mr Wiggins posed a series of Fermi problems.

Fermi questions are named after the physicist and Nobel Prize winner Enrico Fermi who challenged his students to use estimation and reasoning to solve problems that were difficult or impossible to measure. In schools, such problems also pose scenarios that it can be difficult to find a final or accurate answer for example:

> *If all the people in New York joined hands and stretched themselves out in a straight line, how long would it reach?*
>
> *How much space would £1,000,000 worth of £1 coins take up?*
>
> *How many bricks are there in the school building/the street/your city?*

When tackling Fermi problems, children are required to make reasoned assumptions about the situation in order to come up with solution strategies, explaining and justifying what they did when coming up with their approaches. The calculation element is held back, meaning that the focus is therefore shifted away from finding a solution (doing the maths) to a focus on the possible method or strategy used (seeing the maths).

Mr Wiggins began by asking the children how many baked bean tins laid end to end it would take to reach their houses. In order to discourage children from focusing on calculating a solution, he deliberately did not provide the children with any measurements but instead simply asked how they might go about solving the problem. Problems such as these can be useful for holding back the calculation element of problem-solving, giving children the opportunity to focus on strategies and, in Mr Wiggins's class, the removal of the 'doing' element concentrated discussions entirely on the 'seeing' element. Different groups of children came up with different solution strategies. One group decided that they would need to know the distance to each house and the length of the tins and then repeatedly add on one tin length to their total until they reached the total length of the journey home, whilst another eventually concluded that the journey length could be divided by the length of the tin to give the total number needed. All groups also engaged in lengthy discussions about how best the distance to the houses could be measured but the richness of the discussions came in the explaining, reasoning about and justifying their chosen techniques. Following the lesson, the children in Mr Wiggins's class began each afternoon with a five-minute activity discussing and posing possible solution strategies to further Fermi problems: How far do you walk in one year? or, most engagingly, How could you tell which would be taller: 100 monkeys standing on each other's shoulders or 75 humans doing the same?

Task

Try setting some of your own Fermi problems. These could be related to other topics that the class is studying (e.g. for science, how many times do we breathe in a day?) or to recent experiences that they have had (e.g. following a visit to a park, how many blades of grass are growing there?).

The problem with RUCSAC and other problem-solving directions

In an attempt to support children with mathematical problem solving many teachers provide children with a set of rules or instructions to follow. 'RUCSAC' is a commonly used acronym ('**R**ead the question, **U**nderline the key information, **C**hoose the operation, **S**olve the problem, **A**nswer the question, **C**heck your answer'). The 'solve' element is particularly troublesome here as this is the key part of problem-solving and the element that children have difficulty in tackling. Simply asking children to 'solve' does not support or structure the process. Whilst acronyms such as this do contain some useful advice, they often do not support children with the very aspects of problem-solving that they struggle with, for example, What is the key information? or Which operation should I chose and why? As a result, many children simply pick out the numbers and have a go at applying any number operation without really engaging with the mathematical nature of the problem.

Children can also be encouraged to assign certain operations to certain words contained within problems, using key words as clues for which operation to apply. However, as can be seen in the example below this method is not always reliable. Here, the phrase 'more than' is used in problems requiring either addition or subtraction operations:

1. Joe has 5 marbles. Jane has 8 marbles <u>more than</u> Joe. How many marbles does Jane have?
2. Jane has 8 marbles. Joe has 5 marbles. How many marbles <u>more than</u> Joe does Jane have?

If simple, straightforward algorithms or rules cannot be applied to all problem-solving contexts, how can teachers support children in developing the necessary problem-solving strategies required by the National Curriculum to enrich their mathematical learning? Let's have a look at some of the strategies and tweaks used by Mrs Edmonds and her class as an example of the ways in which children can be supported in developing their problem-solving strategies.

Case Study Activity 2 – Tall trees

Original Activity – Using RUCSAC or similar strategies to answer word problems

Rich Tweak – Representing problems using diagrams or resources

During a whole-class discussion on the topic of length, Mrs Edmonds presented her Year 2 class with the following information and problems, asking the children how they might go about answering the questions:

There are two trees growing in a forest. The trunk of one tree is 246 cm tall, and the other is 113 cm tall.
Use this information to answer the following questions:
How much taller is the tall tree than the small tree?
How many of the small trees would you need to be the same height as the tall tree?
What is the total height of the two trees?
If I needed 501-cm length of wood, how many trees would I need to cut down?

Mrs Edmonds had already tweaked a simple problem-solving activity nicely, showing the range of questions which can be asked using only two pieces of information. However, when discussing their ideas with their talk partners the children had only a limited range of strategies to apply. Most could identify that adding the numbers or subtracting one number from another would answer some of the questions but struggled to reason about which questions these strategies could be applied to and to explain why these strategies would work. This indicated that children were failing to engage with the context of the problem fully, making it difficult to see the maths that needed to be done to solve the problem. To assist them with this, Mrs Edmonds gave each pair of children two pieces of paper cut to represent the relative sizes of the trees.

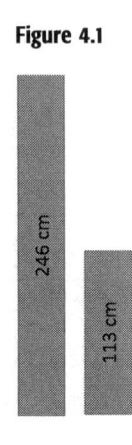

Figure 4.1

Using the model in Figure 4.1, the children were able to manipulate the elements of the problem and so began to visualise the maths that needed to be done. After a short discussion, Archie and Zain reasoned that if they put the two 'tree trunks' next to each other, they could see that they needed to work out the difference in the heights. This suggestion was taken up by the class with some tackling this by counting on whilst others subtracted one height from the other. The resources had enabled the children to see the maths that needed to be done and then to reason about which calculation strategies to apply to achieve this. Further manipulation of the model revealed that placing two small trees on top of each other would help to show many small trees would be needed to make up the height of the taller tree. Rosa explained that she could see that two of these small trees were just shorter than the tall tree, concluding that they would need 'two and a little bit' small trees to make up the length of the tall tree. Mrs Edmonds then asked the class to think about how the model might help them to work out the answer to the last problem, asking the key question, 'How will you represent it?' After some discussion, Paige suggested that they needed another piece of paper to represent the 501 cm needed and that they could line up their models underneath until the lengths matched up.

Verschaffel and De Corte's (1997) research suggests that children become more successful with problem-solving if they can visualise the problem. The small tweak to the activity in providing the children with a model or diagrammatic representation of the problem did not prevent the class from having to engage with the number work involved in solving these problems, but instead, being able to manipulate the representation helped them reason about which number operations were needed and why these were the most suitable approaches. Making the context that the maths is based in visual and apparent through such use of models helps children translate the information provided in the problem into a more easily understood form. Other tweaks that could be used to support children in seeing the maths could be to encourage them to draw pictures of the story in the problem, act it out or use concrete resources to represent the scenario. It is important that children are enabled to view such strategies as working processes. Having non-permanent ways of working such as the paper strips used by Mrs Edmonds here, can not only give children greater insight into the scenarios described in the problem but also more confidence in exploring them.

Task

Take a look at some typical word problems. Which pictures, diagrams, resources or models could be used to support children's understanding of the problem, helping them see the maths which needs to be done:

- There are 10 benches in the playground. Each bench has enough room for 4 people to sit down. How many children could sit on the benches in total?
- The Angel of the North is a large statue in England. It is 20 metres tall and 54 metres wide. Ally makes a scale model of the Angel of the North. Her model is 40 centimetres tall. How wide is her model?
- Cerys bought an ice cream for £1.85 and then a drink for £2.30. If Cerys had £10 to begin with, how much money does she have left now?
- 250 people visited the park one day. 15% came in the morning and 40% in the afternoon. How many people visited the park in the evening?
- By 11 a.m., the hot dog stall had sold 170 hotdogs. They had brought 570 hot dogs with them that day. How many did they now have left?

Case Study Activity 3 – Big and small numbers

Original Activity – Using RUCSAC or similar strategies to answer word problems

Rich Tweak – simplifying using a simpler case

Later Mrs Edmonds was working with a smaller group of Year 2 looking at another problem focused on length and measurement. She presented her group with the following problem:

Two families were each going to visit their grandparents. Beth's family drove 9,867 m to get to her grandparents' house while Ewan's family first walked 3,023 m before having a drink at the café and then continued walking a further 4,976 m to reach his grandparents' house. Who travelled the farthest and by how far?

Initially Mrs. Edmonds asked the group, 'What do you already know?' and 'What else can you find out from that information?' Using these prompts, the group could identify that they knew how far Beth had travelled but struggled to identify anything further. Charlee stated, 'It's too hard for us, we don't do maths with numbers like that'. It appeared that the size of the numbers was too daunting for the group and was preventing them from engaging with the problem and reasoning about forming a strategy to solve it, that is seeing the maths. Mrs Edmonds suggested that they made the numbers easier to work with and adjusted the numbers so that Beth's travelled distance became 10 m and Ewan's 3 m and then 5 m (rounding each of the original distances to the nearest 1,000 and then dividing by 1,000). Immediately Charlee stated, 'Oh that's easy, Ewan went 8 (m) and Beth went 10 (m) so she went the longest', and then used her fingers to count on from 8 to reach 10 and stated that 'Beth went 2 more'. By changing the numbers so that they were easier to work with and were less daunting, Mrs Edmonds had revealed the underlying maths that was required to solve the problem. She then worked with the group, noting the structures used and applying these to work with more complex numbers in the original problem.

Using questioning to support and scaffold problem-solving

We ultimately aim to help children become independent in being able to reason about problem-solving strategies rather than relying on their teachers to tell them what to do. However, it can be difficult to encourage children to embark on a problem if they do not immediately know how to solve it. Barton (2018) discusses the notion of 'goal-free problems'. For many children, the path from the information given in a problem to the answer requires more steps than they can see immediately. Confronted with these problems, the children are unable to make progress as they have no clear strategy to reach the answer. Barton advocates the use of goal-free problems; these are problems where the learner is given the problem information but is not required to find a specific answer (as discussed in the previous chapter). The learner is simply asked to say what they already know or can deduce from the information given. In the process of doing this, the learner is freed from the constraints of looking for a specific answer and the frustration or lack of progress that comes from being unable to find that specific piece of information. This subtle change in the question given to the learners can have a liberating effect on their thinking.

Allowing children time to play with problems, testing out ideas and strategies can help some children see the maths within a problem and therefore what strategies to employ but others require more structure to achieve this which can be drawn out and supported through questioning. In the example problem of children visiting their grandparents described earlier, Mrs Edmonds used starter questions to help the children to enter the problem (clarifying the problem). Questions such as 'What do you already know?' and 'What else can you find out from that information?' can help the children reason about which information they need to identify in order to be able to tackle the problem. This could be simply drawing attention to the detail of the problem or encouraging the children to manipulate the information in some way, focusing thinking in a certain direction. Starter questions can also draw attention to similarities in the type of problem or solution strategy required. Asking 'What have we done before that is like this?' can help children to recall previously used strategies. In Mr Wiggins's lesson, this was apparent when the children used similar strategies to find the difference between numbers. Different types of questions can be used to support problem-solving at different stages of the activity, for example, to help the children see patterns and relationships and therefore to make generalisations and conjectures (see Chapter 5). Typical questions may include asking, 'What is the same or different?' and 'Can the information be grouped in some way, can a pattern be seen?' Reasoning can be challenged by asking, 'What happens if we change . . . ? What if . . . ?', encouraging children to evaluate the validity of their methods.

Children often say that they 'get stuck' during problem-solving activities. This may be because they have used a strategy that has come to a dead-end or that they are unable to see the next step to take. Questioning strategies such as those shown in the following table can be extremely helpful in helping children to overcome this.

'What have you tried?' 'Have you seen anything like this before?' 'Have you thought of another way of doing this?' or 'What else could you try?'	Encourages children to consider a range of approaches and strategies
'What have you discovered?' 'How did you find that out?' 'Why do you think that?' or 'Why did you decide to do it that way?'	Makes the reasoning of others visible
'Who has a different answer?' 'Do we all have the same results (why/why not)?' 'Do we have the same pattern?'	Exemplifies how others are operating or how they arrived at a solution
'Have we found all the possibilities/how do we know?' or 'do you think we found the best solution?'	Challenges the reasoning used

It is important to remember that children will often come up with a strategy that the teacher has not thought of meaning that it can be easy to dismiss such thoughts. Remaining open to a variety of strategies offers further possibilities for reasoning and encourages children to see that in problem-solving, there is often more than one single correct strategy whilst also demonstrating that their suggestions are valued rather than being shut down for being incorrect, thus encouraging further suggestions. Teachers should try to ensure that children are comfortable enough to take risks with this. In a supportive environment, children will gain confidence in explaining and a willingness to try things out.

Jennifer Piggot from Nrich offers some excellent ideas about how such an environment can be achieved. She encourages us to develop problem-solving environments in which it is the children who do most of the talk (recommending that about 70% of the total talk should be done by children). This can be partially achieved by asking open-ended questions and through carefully considering who you are taking answers from and how you respond.

For example, simply replying, 'That's great', could shut down a discussion, but by following up an answer with some of the following examples, children can be encouraged to share and develop ideas. Responding in this way encourages further reasoning and demonstrates that you are interested in and value the ideas provided by children and encourages them to persist and take responsibility for their own learning:

- Are you sure?
- Convince me.
- Show me how you know that.
- I am curious to know why you chose that one.
- I would choose this one. . . . Are we both right?
- What could happen if . . . ?

Likewise, if the same children tend to answer, teachers should consider ways of encouraging all children or all groups to join in, for example by nominating a representative or by posting ideas to an electronic or physical notice board.

Problem-solving is complex and requires time to think. If teachers can resist the urge to finish sentences for children or to hurry them, we can reduce anxiety around discussing strategies and reasoning. However, most important, children also need to feel safe to explore their ideas, knowing that incorrect answers or ideas will be dealt with kindly and even welcomed as a learning tool which allows us to judge how confident the children are and what level/type of support is needed (Piggott, 2008).

Closing questions help children to look back and learn from their experience and should therefore focus on comparing strategies and solutions, revealing relationships and evaluating ideas. Asking the children to work backwards through a problem can encourage them to identify errors. However, at this stage teachers can also focus on meta-cognition or *thinking about their thinking*, helping children to understand the different types of thinking they have used. Teachers could ask children questions which encourage them to evaluate the strategies used, for example, 'Could you do this in two or more ways?' or 'Which is the quickest/easiest way to do this?', demonstrating that simply arriving at the correct answer may not be the end of the process.

Key questions

What do you already know?
What else can you find out from the information that you have?
What have we done before that is like this?
What would happen if . . . ?
Can you draw a picture, use a model, act the problem out or draw a resource to help you to understand the problem?
What have you discovered? How did you find that out?
Why do you think that?
What strategy did you use? Why did you decide to do it that way? Can you think of an alternative strategy? Who used a different strategy? Do you think we used the best strategy/ found the best solution?'

Case Study Activity 4 – Writing word problems

Original Activity – Solving word problems
Rich Tweak – Here's the calculation, write a problem to match

One way to address and assess children's understanding of the processes of problem-solving is to provide them with a calculation and ask them to write a problem to match it or to draw a picture to illustrate the number facts. This not only encourages children to put problems into a real-life context but also encourages them to discuss their approaches and truly exposes their understanding of the operations that they are working with.

Task

Take a look at the following calculations (Figure 4.2). Have a go at writing a problem and drawing a picture to illustrate the following calculations (note that the answers have been provided as doing so encourage the children to focus on seeing the maths rather than doing the maths). As you undertake this, consider the mathematical understanding of the operations that you need to have in place and apply in order to be able to do this.

We have done the first one for you as an example.

Calculation: $5 \times 3 = 15$
Story: Each box of chocolates contains 5 chocolates. If I buy 3 boxes how may chocolates will I have altogether?

Figure 4.2

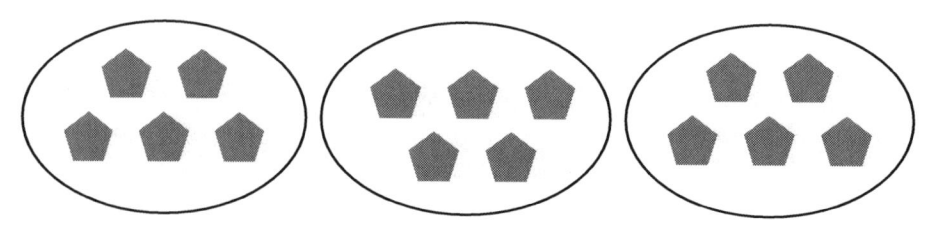

Understanding: I need to know that multiplication represents groups of a quantity and understand multiplication in terms of a repeated addition model. Here I need to know that I have 3 groups of a quantity of 5.

Have a go with these examples:

$24 \div 4 = 6$
$38 - 12 = 26$
$16 + 8 = 24$
$(30 - 12) \div 6 = 3$

Bar Modelling

The use of bar modelling when working with a variety of maths problems is becoming more and more common within UK primary schools, and there is a variety of excellent guidance about how this can be used in classrooms and the advantages that this brings:

> National Centre of Excellence in Teaching Mathematics www.ncetm.org.uk/classroom-resources/ca-the-bar-model/
> Maths No Problem https://mathsnoproblem.com/en/mastery/bar-modelling/
> TES www.tes.com/news/why-every-primary-should-be-using-bar-modelling-and-six-steps-make-it-success

This excellent strategy has one noteworthy advantage in that it helps children to 'see' the maths that needs to be done in order to solve the problems presented to them. A bar model does not necessarily assist with the ultimate calculation but is a powerful tool in revealing what the calculation needs to be done. However, tweaking the activity to turn the more traditional use of bar models around to initially present children with the bar model itself and asking them to write a problem which the model could represent provides an activity which is rich in possibilities. Doing so allows children to invent their own scenarios, possibly basing these on their own wider interests.

In exploring rich mathematical tasks in the book *Even Better Maths*, Ahmed and Williams (2007) state that rich tasks should be accessible to all learners from the start whilst allowing for further challenge and extension. If we take a simple bar chart (Figure 4.3), we can see how this can be the case.

Figure 4.3

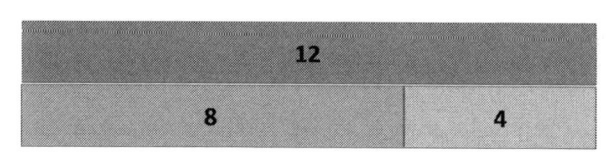

12	
8	4

When faced with the preceding example, a teacher could ask the class to suggest possible addition or subtraction calculations to match the model. However, a richer activity may be to encourage children to suggest word problems instead. Some may suggest simple problems such as 'Elin has £8 and Imogen has £4' (8 + 4 = ?). Be careful to encourage children to include the actual question being asked along with their scenario. They can often forget to do this but is the element which actually reveals their understanding of the model and the problem. Others may extend this thinking, asking, for example, 'I have walked 8 miles, how many more miles do I need to walk to finish my 12-mile walk?' (a more sophisticated 8 + ? = 12). Some may view this in a different way spotting the links to subtraction, for example 'I had 12 sweets but then I ate 4, how many do I have left? (12 − 8 = ?) or again, the more sophisticated 'There were 12 people on the bus, some got off leaving only 4 people remaining. How many people got off the bus?' (12 − ? = 4). By inviting children to discuss the problems that they attach to the given bar models and to share their reasoning about why and how the model represents their problem we encourage them to speculate, prove, explain, interpret and reflecting as described by Ahmed as further benefits of rich tasks. In this way, a class or group discussion of the variety of problems produced by the children and the subsequent thoughts around these offers not only excellent opportunities for the sharing of understanding and reasoning but also assessment opportunities for teachers.

Working in this way can also enrich the learning experience by helping children to see the connections between different elements of maths. In the earlier example, this is evident with addition and subtraction, but bar modelling provides rich opportunities to explore this with other aspects of the curriculum. In the following example, children could view the bar model as a representation of multiplication (e.g. 5 × 7 = 35) or as a division-based problem (35 ÷ 7 = 5). However, the same model could also be applied to a fraction-focused problem, such as 'What is 3 sevenths of 35?' Here the total of 35 has been divided into 7 equal parts, three of these parts totals 15. Seeing the model in this way reveals the relationships among multiplication, division and this aspect of fraction work.

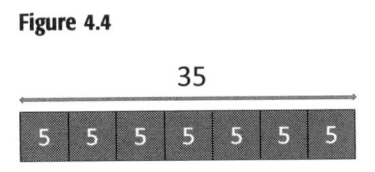

Figure 4.4

| 35 |
| 5 | 5 | 5 | 5 | 5 | 5 | 5 |

As with so many of the rich tasks explored throughout this book teachers can extend thinking by asking, 'What if . . . ?' If we return to our first example (Figure 4.4), what would happen if we changed the number on the top bar to 13 (Figure 4.5)? How would this influence the other numbers in the calculation?

Figure 4.5

| 13 |
| ? | ? |

Or, in the second, 'What if the total represented was 56? What would each part be worth now and how much would 3 sevenths now be?' (Figure 4.6).

Figure 4.6

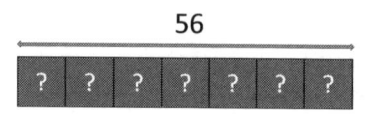

Summary

By their very nature, many mathematical problems already offer rich learning experiences. However, by considering how these activities can be tweaked teachers can deepen understanding not only of the problem-solving process but also of the mathematics associated with this as well as enhancing opportunities for reasoning. By remaining focused on strategies rather than simply the solutions children can be supported in overcoming the common difficulties often experienced with problem-solving and can learn and refine skills that can be applied to problem-solving scenarios across the curriculum. In this way, teachers can avoid the repetitive practice-and-drill approach described by Jo Boaler and experience and a more fluent, creative experience where they are able to express themselves and reason mathematically.

Rich Tweaks – Problem-Solving
Whilst engaging all learners from the start rich mathematical tasks should also allow for further challenge and extension for those children who need it (Ahmed and Williams, 2007). In this way the richness of the learning experience can be tweaked in a number of simple ways:
<ul><li>Reduce the amount of information included in the problem.</li><li>Challenge children to find a variety of solutions (e.g. can you find 3 different solutions? Can you find a solution using, e.g. a square, can you find a solution which does not use addition or does not contain the number 3, etc.)</li></ul>

- Invite learners to make decisions about how to tackle the activity and what mathematics to use and challenge or a variety of solution strategies. You could ask children how many different ways they can find to solve a problem without focusing on the solutions at all.
- Provide children with the answer to an initial problem and ask them/model how to use this information to solve subsequent problems.
- Apply problem-solving scenarios to game-playing.
- Ask 'What would happen if . . . ?' questions – focus on changing different variables each time.
- Find problem-solving activities in real-life contexts (e.g. pricing strategies to make a profit at the tuck shop, the best container design for the tennis balls)
- Use real-life data such as weather data or nutritional information on packaging, timetables and so on.
- Reflect on the strategies that you used – Were they efficient and accurate? Would alternative strategies be better? Why?

References

Ahmed, A. and Williams, H. (2007) *Even Better Mathematics: Looking Back to Move Forward*. London: Network Continuum Education.

Boaler, J. (2015) *The Elephant in the Classroom: Helping Children Learn and Love Maths*. London: Souvenir Press.

Higgins, S. (2003) Parlez-vous mathematics? In enhancing primary mathematics teaching. In *Ian Thompson's Enhancing Primary Mathematics Teaching*. Maidenhead: Open University Press.

Ofsted. (2011) *20 Successful Schools*. London: Ofsted.

Ofsted. (2015) *Better Mathematics Conference Keynote Spring 2015*. Paper presented at the Better Mathematics Conference, Norwich, Norfolk.

Piggot. (2008) *Rich Tasks and Contexts*. Nrich (online). Available from https://nrich.maths.org/5662

Verschaffel, L. and De Corte, E. (1997) Word problems: A vehicle for promoting authentic mathematical understanding and problem solving in the primary school? In T. Nunes and P. Bryant (eds.), *Learning and Teaching Mathematics: An International Perspective*. Hove: Psychology Press.

5
Patterns and variation

In this chapter we examine pattern and variation. Research evidence shows that if children are regularly asked to engage in reasoning about patterns, their broad attainment across mathematics improves (Mulligan et al., 2003; Papic, 2007; Ferrington, 2018). Pattern exploration can be used to develop and reinforce this key curriculum aim of children being able to reason mathematically by following a line of enquiry, conjecturing relationships and generalisations. The chapter begins by exemplifying repeating and growing patterns and explores how they can be used to promote reasoning and mathematical thinking. Following this, a series of examples from the classroom are explored and analysed to consider how patterns and variations might play out within a classroom setting. Through the chapter, we, of course, identify 'rich tweaks' and explain why these would enrich the classroom activity being explored.

In 1975, Marilyn Burns coined the phrase 'pattern is the password to mathematics'. Since then, there have been a number of mathematics educators who have argued vehemently that patterns are the heart and soul of mathematics and should be a central theme within the mathematics curriculum (e.g. Lee, 1996; Zazkis and Liljedahl, 2002; Papic, 2007; Mulligan et al., 2008). Furthermore, examination of young children's mathematical understanding suggests that those children who develop a 'habit' of looking for and manipulating patterns are more able to identify the structure beneath some fundamental areas of mathematics such as number and arithmetic (Mulligan et al., 2003).

Although the current National Curriculum makes little specific mention of patterns (and this is mostly in the non-statutory sections), it does require that in every year group from age 4 to 16, children become able to 'reason mathematically by following a line of enquiry, conjecturing relationships and generalisations' (DfE, 2013, p. 99).

Repeating and growing patterns

A repeating pattern is a pattern with a recognisable repeating cycle of elements (Zazkis and Liljedahl, 2002), whilst a growing pattern is a pattern whereby a relationship between successive terms can be identified (Warren, 2005). These patterns may be made up of numbers, objects, sounds, actions, shapes or images, and your aim should be to explore a range of patterns (both repeating and growing) in order to encourage a versatile and connected habit of looking for patterns in mathematics.

Figure 5.1

Can you identify the repeating cycle in Figure 5.1 for example? Are some patterns easier than others to identify? Why might this be?

Figure 5.2

Can you identify the relationship between successive terms in Figure 5.2? What about Figure 5.3? Might some growing patterns be easier than others to identify? Why might this be?

Figure 5.3

Patterns and variation ◆ 87

Case Study 5.1 – Repeating patterns

Figure 5.4

Figure 5.5

As you can see from these images, repeating patterns with objects are especially accessible and we can begin to interrogate them with children by asking them what they notice about the pattern.

If we take Figure 5.4 for example, we can deepen the questioning by asking things like

1. What comes next in the pattern? How do you know?
2. What will the 10th item in the pattern be? How do you know?

3. Could we extend the pattern in both directions?
4. Is the pattern symmetrical?
5. If we had 21 objects starting with a plain wooden block, how many of them would be red? How do you know? (This last question could open up a conversation in which connections are made to multiples of 3)

Rich Tweak 5.1 – Increasing the complexity

Liljedahl (2004) argues that, in addition to exploring a range of patterns with children, teachers should manipulate the complexity of the patterns that they choose to use. Greater complexity (Figure 5.5) can also be attained through the creation of a pattern with two repeating cycles *of different lengths*.

Look at this pattern Figure 5.6 for example.

Figure 5.6

What is repeating? Follow this repeat right along the line. How long is the repeating cycle?

What else is repeating, though? How long is the cycle of this repeating pattern?

Hopefully you can identify that the shapes are following a repeating pattern which is three in length, working through cube, flat cuboid and upright cuboid. In addition, colours may be used to create a repeating pattern which is four in length, working through yellow, then red, then green and then blue.

A complex pattern such as this one immediately creates an avenue for much richer questioning by the teacher and reasoning by the children. For example, consider the following questions:

> What colour comes next in the sequence (after the blue flat cuboid)? Why?
> What shape should have come before the yellow cube on the left? Why?

If the yellow cube on the left is shape 1, the red flat cuboid shape 2 and so on, answer the following questions:

1. What will be the colour of the 12th shape? Why?
2. In what position will the 4th upright cuboid be? Why?
3. What colour will the 4th upright cuboid be? Why?
4. What will be the colour and shape in position 37? Why?

When designing complex patterns, however, be cautious to ensure that the repeating elements are sufficiently distinct from one another to allow a clear identification of the distinct repeating elements.

Take these two examples (Figure 5.7) – which one more clearly shows the mathematical structure of the pattern?

Figure 5.7

OoOoOoOoOoO

XOXOXOXO

Case Study 5.2 – Growing patterns

Growing patterns, like scaling multiplication, are often overlooked in primary teaching, but they underpin some significant mathematical processes that children need to develop in order to explore algebra competently. But how can we make these seemingly more unfamiliar patterns accessible for primary age children? Let's take a look at an example.

Consider this growing pattern: 7, 10, 13, 16, 19, 22, 25, 28 . . .

We can see that it increases by 3 each time, but how could you support a class to move from this numerical growing pattern towards being able to predict what value the 50th or 100th term would have? How could you support them to express it as an algebraic function?

Rich Tweak 5.2 – Using context/concrete materials to make the growing pattern accessible

Noticing/Conjecturing

Numerical growing patterns are abstract in nature and as such offer little context for children to draw on to support them to notice patterns, reason about patterns and predict how patterns might continue. Let's look at how a teacher, Mr Philips, uses context to explore the above numerical pattern in a Year 5 classroom.

Mr Philips has decided to begin, not with the numerical sequence but instead with a concrete model. He has provided the children with lots of multi-links®, and he asks them to work in pairs to make the three dogs shown in Figure 5.8:

Figure 5.8

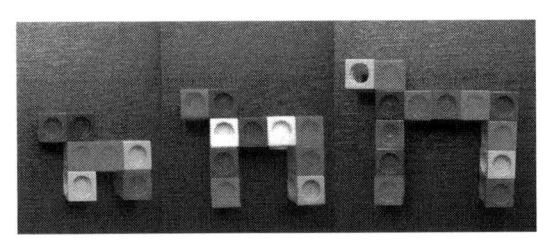

Whilst the children are making the dogs, Mr Philips can hear lots of instances of children 'noticing' things such as 'The next one has two on the back'; 'The head is the same for the next one'. Even without the numerical sequence, the children are beginning to notice the underlying aspects of the pattern. Mr Philips waits until all the children have made all three dogs, challenging quick finishers to predict and make the fourth dog. Mr Philips then asks them to explain what they have noticed. In doing so, Mr Phillips is facilitating the children in noticing the relationships between the dogs — What is changing? What is staying the same?

Mr Philips is aiming for the children to notice the patterns and relationships themselves. He deliberately did not tell them how many cubes to use for each dog (or bit of dog), he instead showed them his pre-made three dogs and them to make them. In the process of making the dogs, the children were immersed in the relationships between dogs and parts of dogs.

The lesson then continues with Mr Phillips questioning the children as they work:

Mr Philips: *What do you think the fourth and fifth dog will look like?* (encouraging them to draw on the relationships they have already noticed in order to predict what might happen next).

Mr Philips: *What will happen to the body? What will happen to the legs? What will happen to the head?* (aiming to help the children realise for themselves that the head stays the same whilst the body and each leg increases by one each time.

Using concrete resources and a context allows Mr Philip and the children to reason together using a shared language (head, body, legs, shoulder, bottom) and a concrete model to point to. This tangible and accessible language is crucial in supporting children to reason about the relationships that they notice.

It is only now, once the children have a full understanding of the relationships between the dogs and their parts, that Mr Philip introduces numbers. Mr Philip asks the children how many cubes are used for the first model, then the second model and then the third, fourth and fifth. The children generate the following numerical growing sequence:

7, 10, 13, 16, 19 . . .

Mr Philips now draws their attention to the numerical pattern and asks them what they notice. The children quickly say that it increases by 3 each time. He asks, 'Why does it increase by 3 each time? What is happening to the dog?' Due to the contextual experience, he is able to prompt the children to make connections between their physical models and the relationships that they have noticed, and the process of adding 3 each time.

Mr Philips is aware that predicting the number of cubes to make the next few dogs can be approached by adding three each time and he guides the children through this, all the time drawing their attention back to physical models to support them in reasoning about how many cubes will be needed for subsequent terms. However, he wants the children to draw on each relationship they have noticed to predict how many cubes will be needed for the 100th dog and ultimately for any dog in the sequence. He draws the children to the problem: Adding three each time is getting time-consuming; let's see if we can use what we know to look at this different way.

Mr Philips now explicitly begins to call the first dog, dog 1 (in algebraic terms we would call this $n = 1$). He asks, 'What does dog 1 have?', pointing to the model and supporting children to explain that dog 1 has 2 cubes for the head, 1 cube for the shoulder, 1 cube for the bottom, 1 cube for the body and 1 cube for each leg; 7 altogether). The dog models are hugely beneficial here as the children can see and point to each section of the dog as they reason about how many cubes it has. He then asks them to explain what dog 2 has and dog 3 and so on. As Mr Philips begins to see solid understanding here, he asks them to predict the number of cubes needed for the 25th dog.

This causes a huge amount of discussion in the classroom as children try to visualise the 25th dog, drawing on the models that they have in front of them. Children are heard to say:

'Well the 25th dog will still have the two for the head, so that's 2'.

'He'll also have only one for the bottom and the shoulder, because they all do'.

'Okay, but what about the legs?' 'Well they are the same length as the number dog it is, so they must be 25 long each! This dog will be a bit wobbly!'

'And the body will also be 25 long' So that's 25 + 25 + 25 and the 4 cubes that stay the same each time . . . 79!'

Mr Philips has deliberately chosen a smallish number here because he can now check with the children by counting up in 3s to the 25th dog. He has also used 25 because it is easy to add together three times to reduce the chance of calculation error and to allow the concept to be revealed without the children becoming overwhelmed by the calculating task. Based on this same premise, Mr Phillips now asks them to predict the number of cubes needed for dog 50 and for dog 100. Again, he is facilitating the children in noticing for themselves the patterns that underlie the predictions that they are making rather than telling them.

Finally, Mr Philips asks the children if they could predict the number of cubes needed for any dog number in the sequence; can they generalise their predictions? After some discussion, in which children were still pointing at their smaller dog models, many children offered the following generalisation:

> Number of cubes = dog number + dog number + dog number + 4
> Which was changed by some to be
> Number of cubes = 3x dog number and then add 4

These children are essentially now expressing the algebraic function of $3n + 4$. However, they have only been able to get to this point through the use of context and concrete materials.

Noticing/Conjecturing

Using patterns to support generalising

The ability to generalise about patterns (in shapes, numbers, data or a range of mathematical situations) is an essential skill which can underpin much wider mathematical understanding and ability.

In fact, Lee (1996, p. 103) states that 'all of mathematics is about generalising patterns'. In this section, we therefore demonstrate how a simple activity can be tweaked and structured to help children develop this skill.

When first looking at a problem, Mason advocates for an entry, attack, review approach (Mason et al., 2010). In order to be able to do this effectively, it is important to provide children with what are known as 'low-threshold high-ceiling tasks'. Such activities present problems in which the task at hand is easy enough to understand so that everyone can access it but offers opportunities for higher or more complex mathematical thinking. 'Entering' such a problem therefore becomes easy as it is clear what needs to be done. Children first start to tackle the problem by playing around with it, experimenting with possible solutions, often referred to as tinkering (see Chapter 6 for further examples).

Case Study 5.3 – 'The magic V'

In the magic V problem (Nrich, https://nrich.maths.org/6274) children are presented with 5 circles arranged into a V shape as shown in Figure 5.9. They are asked to arrange the digits 1 to 5 into the circles (using each digit only once and only placing one digit into each circle) so that the two arms of the V shape add up to the same total.

Figure 5.9

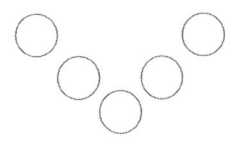

When children first encounter this problem, they may tackle it randomly, placing numbers into the circles until they arrive at a solution. Such trial-and-error approaches can often be effective but do not move mathematical understanding or the development of problem-solving skills forward. If work on the problem stops once an initial solution has been found, then further opportunities for reasoning are lost. By encouraging children to use their solutions to suggest more general rules about how the problem can be tackled teachers can help children develop skills of reasoning around generalising.

Rich Tweak 5.3 – Finding patterns in solutions

Exploring/Noticing/Conjecturing

Children are naturally curious and so often look for patterns and connections. This was nicely demonstrated by a group of Year 4 children who began to notice similarities between their solutions to the magic V problem. For example, they noted that whilst the number 3 was often the central circle the number 2 was never in that position and that whilst the number 5 was often paired with the number 1 in the arms of the V, it was never paired with the 4. It is this noticing of pattern which is the first step in richer mathematic thinking, leading towards the 'conjecturing relationships and generalisations' referred to in the National Curriculum.

Whilst spotting patterns is an important first step, it is understanding why the pattern works and the formulation of an argument, reasoning why the pattern works that is important. This begins with making a conjecture. We conjecture something when we are not sure of something and have to guess, meaning that a conjecture is a mathematical statement or idea that has not yet been proved. In this example, the children began to use the patterns that they had spotted to conjecture possible rules for solving the magic V problem stating that:-

'There should always be a 3 in the middle'.

'In the arms, a big number should be paired with a small number'.

This type of thinking may not come naturally to some children, and as Mason et al., (2010) states, these skills need to be nurtured and developed within mathematics lessons such as through the careful use of questions and prompts, whole class or group discussions or teachers modelling conjecturing behaviour. For this to be done successfully, there must be a classroom ethos whereby children feel safe to share their reasoning about these ideas and to be wrong at times. When such statements are made teachers therefore need to respond appropriately to encourage further mathematical exploration. Let's look at the magic V example again and the child who conjectured that 'there should always be a 3 in the middle'. Rather than replying, 'No, that's incorrect', the teacher here replied, 'What would happen if there was a 5 in the middle?' The child then continued to work on the problem using this as a starting point and found that their original conjecture was incorrect but noticed that there was always a 1, 3 or 5 in the centre circle.

Rich Tweak 5.4 – Putting conjectures to the test; why does it work/not work?

Conjecturing/explaining

Simply stating and accepting a conjecture without testing it and establishing if it is always true again limits the potential for developing mathematical thinking. The opportunities for reasoning lie in the further development and exploration of the problem, testing the conjecture and reasoning about why it works.

By noticing and describing a pattern, children can identify the 'general case', enabling them to make a generalisation, which is always correct and can therefore be used for any unknown example. In our case study, the children established that 'there should always be an odd number in the middle' and tested this to establish that it was always true. However, there is often an important step that is missed at this stage which is reasoning about why the pattern works and why the general rule can be applied. Such thoughts challenged the children in our case study and prompted much discussion. Eventually they reasoned that their generalisation worked because there were '3 odd numbers, and if one arm had two of these numbers and the other only one they could not be equal (one would add up to an even number and one odd)'. This led them to further generalise that each of the arms must contain an odd and an even number. If we understand an idea well enough to reason about our generalisations in this way, we have probably mastered the concept, one of the key processes in the development of mastery of mathematics.

Rich Tweak 5.5 – Transferring thinking

'Reasoning'

Having worked on one specific example, a key skill in moving reasoning about generalisations forward is to be able to transfer what you have learnt in that one example to another, new example. Finding strategies which will always work is a key principle of a generalisation. To encourage this the children were asked to repeat the problem but this time using the digits 2 to 6. At first, the children placed an odd number into the central circle, following their earlier generalisation but soon noticed that this strategy now did not work, so they looked back to their previous reasoning about why this generalisation had worked for the first example (i.e. thinking about how many odd and even numbers they had in the set of numbers that they were working with).

1, 2, 3, 4, 5 = three odd numbers.   2, 3, 4, 5, 6 = two odd numbers

Kate noticed that they now had more even numbers than odd, reasoning that if they now put an odd number in the middle circle only one of the arms would have an odd number in it. She redid the problem by placing an even number in the central circle, finding that this worked. Having transferred thinking from one example to another the group were able to state what will always be true surmising that 'if you have

> more add than even numbers an odd number goes in the middle, but if you have more even than odd and even number goes in the middle'.

Patterns and procedural variation

In this section, we examine procedural variation (sometimes known as intelligent practice), what it is, how is linked to pattern and how it can be used to support children's reasoning in developing a deeper understanding of processes (procedures).

If we think of patterns as relationships with some kind of regularity between the different elements, we can begin to understand why spotting patterns is important for understanding number operations. For example, noticing that when we add 5 to an 8, or any number ending in an 8, the answer will end in a 3 helps us understand something about the nature of the number 5 and how we can use this as an addition strategy.

> 8 + 5 = 13 (8 + 2 + 3), 28 + 5 = 13 (28 + 2 + 3), 148 + 5 = 153 (148 + 2 + 3), etc.

Procedural variation provides us with an opportunity to use pattern spotting to reveal the structure of the mathematics being explored using a carefully designed set of questions that will draw children's attention to a particular aspect of mathematics.

> **Case Study 5.4: Multiplication by 10, 100, 0.1**
>
> Despite the rich opportunities that working with patterns offers for establishing understanding, much of the work presented in textbooks or worksheets is random, a series of unrelated questions on a common theme, making pattern spotting extremely difficult. In the following,

there is little, if any relationship between the questions asked. This means that what is learnt from question 1 is difficult to apply to question 2 and so on. Here, the questions are unrelated, and the task becomes focused on calculating an answer rather than consolidating understanding of the concept or strategy being used to calculate.

1   3 × 100
2   16 × 10
3   4 × 0.1
4   836 × 1000

Rich Tweak 5.4 – Ordering calculations to reveal underlying patterns and concepts (procedural variation)

Noticing

Rather than a using a random selection of calculations, teachers can present questions in a systematic manner so they generate a pattern. This helps illustrate the essential features of a concept or idea. In this way, procedural variation is not the same as simply providing a variety of questions but rather narrows the focus, using a carefully thought out set of developing questions which have been purposefully designed and ordered to develop and exemplify a pattern and therefore draw out the children's understanding of a specific concept. Our set of questions now becomes

1   4 × 8 =
2   40 × 8 =
3   400 × 8 =
4   4,000 × 8 =
5   40,000 × 8 =

6   0.4 × 8 =
7   0.04 × 8 =

Let's take a look at an example used by Mr Langley in his classroom. Initially the children were presented with some direct instruction to help them calculate 4 × 8. Using the representation below to support their thinking the children established that there were 8 groups of 4 (Figure 5.10).

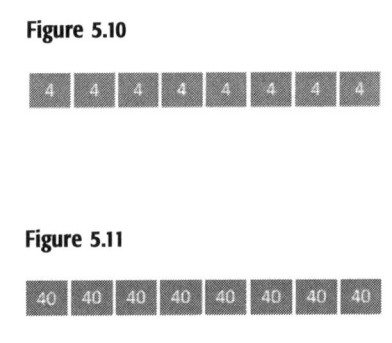

Figure 5.10

| 4 | 4 | 4 | 4 | 4 | 4 | 4 | 4 |

Figure 5.11

| 40 | 40 | 40 | 40 | 40 | 40 | 40 | 40 |

And further reasoning that 40 x 8 would be 8 lots of 40 (Figure 5.11).

A key idea in mathematics is being able to identify similarities and differences (Haylock, 2018), and this can be extended to pattern work. By asking the children, 'What changed?' Mr Langley focused the children on the variation between the outcomes (i.e. the numbers are bigger by a factor of 10), and by asking, 'What stays the same?', he helped the children focus on the consistencies between the procedures (i.e. the number of groups stayed the same). In this example, the systematically ordered questions therefore enabled the children to identify a pattern emerging in their answers and reason about the relationship between the procedures. The children reasoned that the answers were increasing by a factor of 10 each time as the number of items in each group was bigger by a factor of 10 each time (4, 40, 400). This directly reflects the central idea of teaching with variation which is to highlight the essential features of a concept or idea through varying the non-essential features (i.e. the number multiplied), helping consolidate understanding of the underlying concept. Practice therefore becomes intelligent by using what has been learnt and established in an earlier example rather than mechanical.

Rich Tweak 5.5 – Using and applying patterns to predict

Reasoning

Identifying a pattern and being able to reason about why this pattern has emerged is a rich mathematical experience for children. However, reasoning can still be developed further through a simple tweak to the activity.

Working with patterns helps us to define what has come before and to use this to predict what will come next. Procedural variation develops this by using movement between one question and the next, encouraging children to use *what they know about the previous calculation to work out what they don't know about the next*. Drawing on this concept, Mr Langley then challenged the children to solve a series of further, related calculations (4,000 × 8, 40,000 × 8, etc.) asking, 'How did the answer to the last question help you answer this one?' Establishing a firm understanding of the pattern ensured that the children were able to use this to predict and reason about the answers to these subsequent questions demonstrating a developing understanding of the concept being explored.

In our example, a child may simply conclude that when multiplying by 10 one should just add a 0 to the end of the original number. The addition of the calculations 0.4 × 8 and 0.04 × 8 used next by Mr Langley disproved this and therefore helped lead to understanding about

> place-value position. Mr Langley had carefully selected the examples he used and introduced these at specific times to help children see the intended connections and to support them in spotting patterns and making correct generalisations, revealing the structure of the mathematics being explored. In this way he avoided a focus on simple mechanical repetition, instead providing systematic opportunities for noticing and reasoning. Watson and Mason (2006) refer to this as using variation to structure sensemaking.

Summary

Both Threlfall (1999) and Papic (2007) argue vehemently that mere exposure to patterns is insufficient; teachers need to plan the task and questions that they will ask carefully, in order to ensure deep and meaningful understanding. Furthermore, Threlfall (1999) argues that teachers should also carefully plan the order of their questions to scaffold an increasing understanding of the pattern in question. Through the case studies examined in this chapter, we have seen that the teacher is crucial in facilitating mathematical thinking through careful task design, observation of evolving understanding and targeted questioning that seeks to draw children's attention to patterns, relationships and underlying mathematical structures.

As with so many approaches to teaching maths, the deeper, rich learning comes through the dialogue that accompanies the tasks. Asking *'What do you notice?'* gives the opportunity to focus on the key teaching points for the concept or problem and supports the children making in generalisations. Furthermore, asking, *'How did you work it out?'* opens up opportunities to explore the inherent pattern and process, picking up misconceptions or errors and giving you the chance to deepen children's understanding by breaking down those processes and applying them to other problems. Children can be further challenged with the question, 'Can you find any exceptions to our pattern and rule?'

Key questions/statements:

What is the same? What is different?
What has changed?
What do you notice?
How does... help you to answer...?
What do you notice about...? How might it help?
Can you find any exceptions to our pattern and rule?
Where is the mistake in this pattern? how do you know?
What is repeating? How do you know?
What will be in position...? How do you know?
Why is there a, for example, 3/square in position 12? Is this correct?
What can you tell me about the pattern?
What would happen if...?

Rich Tweaks – Four operations	
Standard Activity	**Rich Tweak Activity**
Random selection of calculations 264 − 84 = 264 − 188 = 260 − 80 = 264 − 180 = 264 − 88 =	Carefully order the set of calculations given so that the children's thinking and understanding of procedure are developed throughout the exercise. Consider how this narrowing the focus on procedure and process rather than on repeated number crunching

	+	−	×	÷
	523 + 400 = 423 + 500 = 323 + 600 = 223 + 700 = 123 + 800 =	260 − 80 = 264 − 84 = 264 − 88 = 264 − 180 = 264 − 188 =	6 × 8 = 6 × 80 = 6 × 800 = 60 × 8 = 600 × 8 = 60 × 80 =	36 ÷ 7 = 37 ÷ 7 = 38 ÷ 7 = 39 ÷ 7 = 40 ÷ 7 =

Rich Tweaks – Problem-solving	
Standard Activity	**Rich Tweak Activity**
Word problems	Provide children with the answer to an initial problem and ask them/model how to use this information to solve subsequent problems. A bus can hold 34 people. How many people can 6 busses hold? How many people could travel on 7 busses/4 busses/60 busses/12 busses? If the product of 24 and 15 is 360, what is the product of 24 and 16? If the product of 24 and 5 is 120, what is the product of 24 and 25? Can you explain how you know?

Rich Tweaks – Problem-solving	
Standard Activity	**Rich Tweak Activity**
Answering calculations	Provide the children with a solution. Ask them to establish a series of possible calculations which would give this solution and explain how they are related to each other. The answer is 420. What is the question? (e.g. 500–80; 490–70; 480–60; 470–50 etc)

Rich Tweaks – Factors	
Standard Activity	**Rich Tweak Activity**
What are the factors of random numbers (e.g. 10, 24, 15)	How can the factors of 10 help you to find the factors of 20? How can the factors of 12 help you to find the factors of 36? Find the factors of 8, 16 and 24.

Rich Tweaks – Fractions	
Standard Activity	**Rich Tweak Activity**
Finding fractions of random numbers	1/3 of 60
	2/3 of 60
	1/3 of 6
	2/3 of 6
	1/3 of 600
	2/3 of 600
	1/3 of 120
	2/3 of 120
	2/3 of 1200
	1/3 of 1/6

References

Burns, M. (1975) *The I Hate Mathematics Book*. Boston: Little, Brown and Company.

Department for Education (DfE). (2013) *National Curriculum in England: Framework Document*. London: Department for Education.

Ferrington, B. (2018) Pattern, the password to mathematics: Cracking the code with Year 2. *Australian Primary Mathematics Classroom*, 23(4), pp. 4–9.

Haylock, D. (2018) *Mathematics Explained for Primary Teachers* (6th Edition). London: Sage.

Lee, L. (1996) An initiation into algebraic culture through generalization activities. In N. Bednarz, C. Kieran and L. Lee (eds.), *Approaches to Algebra: Perspectives for Research and Teaching*, pp. 87–106. Dordrecht: Kluwer Academic Publishers.

Liljedahl, P. (2004) Repeating pattern or number pattern: The distinction is blurred. *Focus on Learning Problems in Mathematics*, 26(3), pp. 24–42.

Mason, J., Burton, L. and Stacey, K. (2010) *Thinking Mathematically* (2nd Edition). Harlow: Pearson Education.

Mulligan, J., Mitchelmore, M., Kemp, C., Marston, J. and Highfield, K. (2008) Encouraging mathematical thinking through pattern and structure: An intervention in the first year of schooling. *Australian Primary Mathematics Classroom*, 13(1), pp. 10–15.

Mulligan, J. T., Prescott, A. and Mitchelmore, M. C. (2003) Taking a closer look at young students' visual imagery. *Australian Primary Mathematics Classroom*, 8(4), pp. 23–27.

Papic, M. (2007) Promoting repeating patterns with young children – more than just alternating colours. *Australian Primary Mathematics Classroom*, 12(3), pp. 8–13.

Threlfall, J. (1999) Repeating patterns in the primary years. In A. Orton (ed.), *Pattern in the Teaching and Learning of Mathematics*, pp. 18–30. London: Cassell.

Warren, E. (2005) Young children's ability to generalise the pattern rule for growing patterns. In H. L. Chick and J. L. Vincent (eds.), *Proceedings of the 29th Annual Conference of the International Group for the Psychology of Mathematics Education*, Vol. 4, pp. 305–312. Melbourne: PME.

Watson, A. and Mason, J. (2006) Seeing an exercise as a single mathematical object: Using variation to structure sense-making. *Mathematical Thinking and Learning*, 8(2), pp. 91–111.

Zazkis, R. and Liljedahl, P. (2002) Generalization of patterns: The tension between algebraic thinking and algebraic notation. *Educational Studies in Mathematics*, 49(3), pp. 379–402.

6
Mathematical investigations, systematic thinking and finding all the possibilities

In this chapter, we explore ways of engaging children in investigative mathematical thinking. We continue with our notion of 'rich tweaks' and explore ways of turning routine tasks into tasks that involve more investigative thinking. We focus specifically on tasks that involve systematic thinking and those that require the children to find all the possibilities (and to show that they have found them all).

Introduction

Maths is often viewed as a subject where answers are right or wrong. This can lead to anxieties about performance or competence (Boaler, 2009). Working with investigations which have more than one outcome can help address this preconception, encouraging a more explorative approach. One of the features of a good investigation is that it does not have a specific end-point or final answer; ideally, the children engaged in the investigation are able to ask further questions so as to extend the investigation further. An article published by the Nrich team in 2013 highlighted the importance of mathematical activities in which there are several paths to the 'answer' and in which children have a sense of agency. The Nrich team terms mathematical activities in which every child can make a start but which allow for different children to take the activity in a direction of their choosing 'low-threshold, high-ceiling' tasks. It summarises them as follows:

> Low Threshold High Ceiling tasks are designed to have lots of built-in extension opportunities, so that there are harder questions to be asked and more challenging problems to solve. This means that all learners can potentially reach a point where they don't immediately know what to do next, and they can start to develop their resilience and learn fruitful strategies for making progress when they feel as if they've come up against a brick wall.
>
> Nrich (2013)

In the next section, we introduce an activity which could initially be considered as a vehicle for developing children's calculation skills but which, with a few 'rich tweaks', can become a useful vehicle for the development of children's mathematical thinking. We would like you to follow this investigation along with us (you'll need a pencil and paper, and possibly a calculator) so that you can get a sense of what doing an investigation 'feels' like. Following this, we look at two case studies so you can see what investigations might look like when carried out with children.

The task–number chains (we strongly suggest that you engage in this investigation along with us. To do this you will need a cup of tea (optional) and a pencil and paper).

There are two rules:

If a number is even, halve it
If a number is odd, multiply by 3 and add 1.

You (or the children) choose a starting number, apply the preceding rules to generate a new number, to which the rules are then applied. This generates a chain of numbers. Before you (or they) do this, it is important to model the process.

For example, let's take 6 as a starting number. Six is even, so it is halved to make 3. Three is odd, so it is multiplied by 3 and 1 is added, making 10. Ten is even, so it is halved to make 5 and so on and so on. This might be recorded like this:

$6 \rightarrow 3 \rightarrow 10 \rightarrow 5 \rightarrow$

If you have not come across this investigation before, you might like to put the book down, make a cup of tea and spend an enjoyable five minutes exploring what happens as you continue that chain onwards. We are deliberately not saying what will happen; that is for you to find out. Once you feel that this particular chain has come to a natural end, stop and read on.

One of the keys to developing children's investigative skills is to encourage them not to stop when they feel they have found an 'answer'. In the number chain that you just explored, you (hopefully) found that the chain came to a natural end; you couldn't really go any further. You might like to consider how you would support or encourage children to take this little investigation further.

Rich Tweak 6.1: Getting the children to ask their own questions about an investigation is one of the keys to extending the investigation

In the earlier number chain example, we began with the number 6 and followed it through to its natural conclusion.

Thinking about this, are there any particular questions that you might have about this? Make a note of them before you read on.

Here are a few of ours:

Do all starting numbers lead to the same outcome?
If so, do larger numbers lead to longer chains?
If not, which numbers don't lead to chains that resolve themselves?
Are there any 'special' numbers which lead to very short chains? Why?
Which numbers generate especially long chains? Why?

You (and especially the children you teach) may well have further questions. In the course of their investigations, they may find particularly interesting numbers (e.g. we found that 27 was an interesting starting number; you may want to begin a chain with 27 and see what happens).

We hope that you have spent an enjoyable couple of minutes exploring what happens when you begin with particular numbers. You may have begun to formulate some general rules. For example,

If you start with an odd number, the chain always . . .

If you start with a small number, the chain always . . .

The use of the word *always* is very helpful for getting children to explore further and lends itself to justification and proof (see Chapter 5) for more information on these areas of mathematical thinking.

Rich Tweak 6.2 – Asking 'What happens if . . . ?' questions

As noted earlier, investigations differ from problems in that they do not have a definite end-point, although there are points in an investigation, which feel like a natural place to finish. We have reached one such place, but there is scope for extending this particular investigation further. We have noted at other points in the book (see the case studies further on in this chapter), that the question, 'What happens if . . . ?' is one of the most powerful that you (or, ideally, your children) can ask in a maths lesson. Investigations are often excellent places for this kind of questioning.

In our number chains investigation, once the children have become confident with exploring the chains and what happens with different starting numbers, they may feel ready to ask, 'What happens if we change the rules?'

As a teacher, giving over this amount of control to the children may feel a little scary. After all, you cannot be sure what the children will decide to do with the rules. You may wish to begin by suggesting some 'What happens if . . . ?' questions. It may be that the rules take them off in a direction that doesn't lead to a learning outcome that you had intended. The thing to remember is that it is the process of exploring and being able to articulate what they have learned from that process, which is the key learning objective here. So, in this particular investigation, it is likely that the children will find out something about odd and even numbers, but other investigations may well lead them to explore other areas of mathematics.

So what kinds of rule changes might be interesting with this particular activity? Spend a few minutes exploring the effect of these changes:

Even – halve the number and add 1

Odd – add 3

Once you have spent a couple of minutes exploring the effects of these rule changes, try changing the rules again and exploring what happens.

As noted previously, you may find it slightly uncomfortable to hand over a certain amount of control over the investigation to the children. If the children in your class are not used to working in this way, you may well need to provide some structure to the activity initially, for example, by working together as a whole class on the investigation, possibly following a rule change suggested by one of the children. This may then give them the confidence to change the rules for themselves.

Recording the Children's Thinking

One of the nice aspects of investigative mathematics is that it is not encumbered by the large amount of recording that may accompany other mathematical activities. However, we do recommend that the children are systematic in recording what they find out. Some kind of pro forma, like the one that follows, might be useful, partly to provide you with assessment information and partly for the children to remember what they did and learned and as a way of sharing ideas and outcomes among the children.

While this doesn't involve a huge amount of recording, it does encourage the children to do more than simply play aimlessly with the rules. Having made one change and observed its effects, they might then go on to suggest a further change to 'fix' or alter one of the effects they had observed. In the case highlighted earlier, the children might be encouraged to think about how to change the rule so that you do get some odd numbers back in the chain (e.g. changing the even rule to 'double and add 5').

Name of Investigation: Number Chains			
What I did	What I thought would happen	What actually did happen	Why did this happen
Changed the even rule to 'double and add 2' Kept the odd rule to ×3 and +1	The chains would take longer to come to an end as the numbers would get a bit bigger.	The chains go on forever. As soon as you hit an even number, they just get bigger and bigger.	I think it happened because when you double an even number, it stays even. If you add two to an even number, it stays even, so you never get any odds.

Case Study 6.1 – Finding all the possibilities

Now that you have had a go at engaging in an investigation, we will look at two case studies of investigations in the classroom. They will be used to exemplify two key considerations when facilitating investigations: 'finding all the possibilities' and 'working within parameters'. Through these case studies, we will look at how to take such a task and open it (or give it a 'rich tweak') to give it a higher ceiling with multiple pathways and end-points. We also explore how each teacher encourages reasoning and conjecturing whilst supporting the children to follow a line of enquiry and test out ideas.

Finding all possibilities investigations require that children do not finish an investigation once they have found a single solution. Instead, they encourage further examination and systematic working to find all the solutions that could be possible. At first it may seem that problems which require children to find all possibilities do not fit with our definition of *mathematical investigations* in that they could have a definite end-point (i.e. a definitive number of possibilities). However, this type of mathematical work is almost entirely focused on the process of investigation and offers opportunities for exploration, divergent thinking and therefore reasoning.

Let's look in more detail at an example from a Year 1 classroom in which Gareth is the teacher. Gareth and his Year 1s are considering the following problem:

> Original Activity
> Izzy would like to buy a biscuit which costs 6p.
> Which coins should Izzy use to pay for the biscuit?

Considering which coins to use to pay for an item is a common classroom activity, for example in a role-play area or 'buying' items from a shop/ice cream menu and so on. Children can share their answers, but this only offers opportunities for explaining thinking rather than for more sophisticated reasoning. If this activity is to be done in a way that leads to richer opportunities for reasoning, the teacher will not stop once a child has given a correct answer but will rather continue to explore the problem until all possibilities have been found.

Rich Tweak 6.3 – Finding all the possibilities

Reasoning

This task is quickly and easily tweaked to be richer by opening it up to be a 'find all the possibilities' task. However, Gareth needs to think carefully about how he will guide his class through this investigation in order to draw their attention to key features of mathematical thinking.

Izzy would like to buy a biscuit which costs 6p.

How many different ways of paying for this biscuit are there?

First, Gareth has deliberately used numbers that are well within the grasp of the children in his class. When encouraging mathematical thinking, we need investigations to be numerically accessible; this will allow the children to see the underlying concepts rather than become overwhelmed by the calculations. Additionally, having only a small number of possible results means that problem is easy to manage; that is we can easily prove by exhaustion that we have found all possibilities.

Let us now look at how this task developed through Gareth's careful teaching:

Gareth took answers from various members of the class, encouraging exploration, and recorded these in a haphazard way.

1p + 1p + 1p + 1p + 2p; 2p + 2p + 2p; 1p + 5p; 1p + 2p + 2p +1p

After recording a few solutions, Gareth stopped the class and asked, 'Hang on a minute – you can't all be right, can you?' The children were encouraged to check the calculations and reasoned that they were all correct – the cost of the biscuit remained the same – but that they could use different coins (different solutions) to pay, encouraging them to see that there could be more than one way to solve the challenge, an important step for some. Gareth began to record more solutions on the board, carefully selecting those which had already been provided but where the coins were presented in a different order in order to encourage further opportunities to reason.

5p + 1p; 2p + 2p + 1p + 1p; 2p + 1p + 1p + 1p + 1p

Before Gareth could go any further, he was interrupted by Lily, who said, 'But we've already got that one' (pointing to 1p + 5p). Gareth paused the activity and encouraged the children to reason about what was the same and what was different about the solutions that they had found so far.

As Barclay and Barnes (2013) state, considering equivalence helps children have insights about their maths beyond the procedural. Here, the children initially discussed the fact that they had the same coins in different orders but reasoned that as they gave the same totals, they had replicated an answer (and therefore had unknowingly explored the commutative law of addition). It is only through reasoning about such equivalences that children will be able to sort and group the solutions that they come up; without such thinking, they will not be able to work through the challenge systematically.

Exploring

The discussion then moved on to consider if they had found all the possible ways of paying. Gareth encouraged the children to begin to think systematically by asking, 'If we want to make a list of the different solutions, which one would be a good one to start with?'

Working systematically, ordering and grouping possible answers according to characteristics helps identify patterns and techniques for finding further solutions. However, children may not be inherently able to work in a systematic way such as this and will need to be taught and practise these skills over time if they are to develop these important cross-curricular and life skills. Some investigations have more obvious starting points (e.g. here, the value of the coins), while others will be less obvious (e.g. problems involving colours). However, establishing a starting point is important if the rest of the work is to be systematic. Systematic listing offers much more sophisticated opportunities for reasoning than simply working out one single solution as illustrated by George, who reasoned that he would start with the 'biggest coin [meaning the highest value, the 5p] because its easiest to add to', adding that 'there's only one way to do it with a 5p there isn't another way 'cause if you add anything else it will be more than 6p'.

Children also need to be able to reason that answers haven't been missed. With this in mind, Gareth turned the attention to the solutions containing a 2p and asked, 'How do we know that we haven't missed any? Having a system ensures that you don't leave any options out, and so here Gareth encouraged the children to look for patterns (another of Barclay and Barnes's big ideas).

James and Richie noticed that the first solution here contained one 2p and the second two 2ps. They used this evidence to suggest a third option of three 2ps. Gareth added this idea to the board and continued to add a further solution of four 2ps, much to the children's outrage, who told him that added up to too much! Gareth used this point to conclude that they must have now found all the possible ways of paying for the biscuit.

5p + 1p; 2p + 1p + 1p + 1p + 1p
2p + 2p + 1p + 1p
2p + 2p + 2p
~~2p + 2p + 2p + 2p~~

However, the children had other ideas. Using the system being modelled to them helped them see that there could be further possibilities, namely those starting with 1p. Again, focusing on what was the same and different between the solutions starting with 1p and those already recorded, the group eventually decided that there was only one further solution to add to the list;

5p + 1p; 2p + 1p + 1p + 1p + 1p; 1p + 1p + 1p + 1p + 1p + 1p
2p + 2p + 1p + 1p
2p + 2p + 2p

Recording solutions in an efficient way enabled the children to persevere with the challenge, to know when all possibilities are found and to check for repeats of possibilities. Gareth then concluded the activity by referring back to the original problem: 'How many different ways of paying 6p for the biscuit did we find? 'Which way uses the most/fewest coins?

Rich Tweak 6.4 – Adapting the problem

Further exploring

At this point, it may appear that the investigation has been concluded. However, there are various ways in which this could be opened up to promote further exploration and reasoning. Further rich opportunities to explore could be:

- How many solutions there might be if the biscuit cost 7p? Would there be just one more solution?
- Is there a pattern between the cost of the biscuit and the number of possible solutions (does the number of ways to pay go up by the same amount as the cost of the biscuit?)
- What would happen if we had a 3p or a 4p coin?
- How many ways of solving this using 2 coins are there? 3 coins? 4 coins and so on?

Ideas such as these can also be used to give children different exit points from the investigation providing different levels of challenge.

Reasoning with non-examples

In extending the investigation beyond the original scenario, children can draw on the methods and ways of thinking that developed in the original problem and apply these patterns, generalisations and systems of working to the new case. One excellent rich tweak to the activity which can provide scope for more sophisticated reasoning is to ask what are all the possible ways of NOT making 6p (i.e. which combinations of 1p, 2p and 5p coins would not give us a total of 6p). Using this approach opens up opportunities for reasoning with children needing to explain why certain combinations of coins would not be suitable; for example we cannot use 6 coins or more because even if we only use 1p pieces this would make a total of 6p. If children struggle to view the problem in this way, they can be supported with some prompt questions such as 'Could we use a 5p and a 2p? Why/why not?' 'Why could I not use more than one 5p coin?' and so forth. The principles and practices applied to finding all the possibilities could also be applied to finding all the non-possibilities.

Case Study 6.2 – Working within parameters

The previous example contained innate, contextual 'rules' or parameters for the children to work within; they could only use coins. This created parameters to the problem that prevented them using 3p as an amount, for example (assuming that they already had a secure understanding of coins). Coins are an ideal way to implicitly create parameters such as these, but children also need to become fluent in investigating problems in which the 'rules' or parameters are laid down at the outset. The following case study explores this further.

Original Activity – Can you put the chocolates in the box while keeping to the rules?

Imagine that you have a chocolate box with 6 sections (in a 2x3 array) that you need to place 6 chocolates into (see Figure 6.1). Each box has to have 3 mid grey sweets (because these are the most popular), 2 light grey sweets and 1 dark grey sweet. To make them look as good as possible you cannot put two colours in adjacent sections.

Figure 6.1

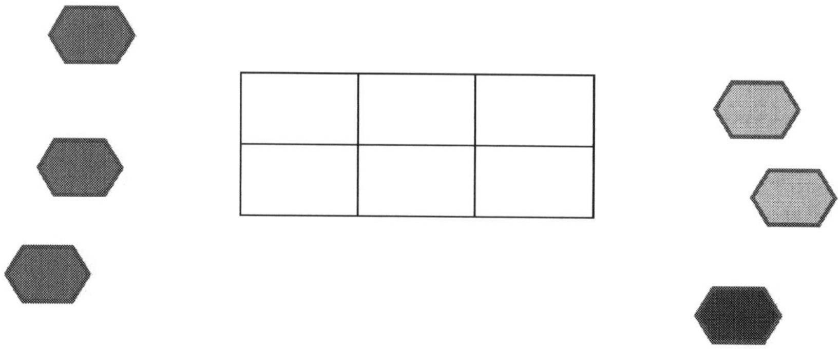

120 ◆ Investigations and systematic thinking

In this activity, colours and spatial arrangements are used rather than numbers. Varying your investigations in this way will help pupils make connections and become more fluent in drawing on their developing mathematical thinking across a range of situations. What also makes this investigation different to the coins one is that the 'rules' or parameters of the problem are laid down explicitly: the size and arrangement of the box; the colour and number of the sweets and the rules about how sweets can be placed.

Hopefully, your immediate thought beyond this is 'Why stop at one solution? Let's find all the possibilities! So your first rich tweak would be the following:

Rich Tweak 6.5 – How many ways can the chocolates be arranged in the chocolate box while always keeping to the rules.

Exploring

Just as we did before, let's look at how it might develop in the classroom. In parallel to the problem earlier, this activity draws directly on context and can therefore be explored by beginning with a story and using resources. The teacher here, Lisa, has provided her Year 2 children with a range of egg boxes and crumbled-up paper of different colours (see Figure 6.2). She could also have used multilink® cubes or counters to represent the sweets.

Figure 6.2

She first explains the problem to the children and then asks them to discuss how we might begin to investigate. The children discuss it in pairs before Lisa brings them back together. While they discuss it, Lisa tries to spot children who are deliberately working within the parameters of the investigation. For example, she overhears Maddie saying, 'No, Tom, we have to get the right number of each colour', and she also notices that most children have reached for the 2×3 egg boxes rather than the 2×2, 2×5 or 2×6 ones. Lisa takes all of this information in and then draws the children back together.

At this point, the investigation is still evolving, but this first opportunity to talk amongst themselves has created a 'low threshold' (Nrich, 2011) access point; all children can begin to access the problem. Lisa then keeps the children progressing together (per the guidance in the National Curriculum) by asking those children whom she noticed making logical choices about the parameters of the problem to explain what they were doing and why. Lisa also asks 'not' questions; for example, Why didn't you choose the larger egg box? Why didn't you have 4 red sweets? With careful questioning directed at children whom she notices have made deliberate choices around the parameters, Lisa can draw out and exemplify the first few rules of the problem – the chocolate box size and layout and the numbers and colours of sweets. In this way, all children are progressing together through the problem and are being encouraged to notice the parameters for themselves.

Noticing

After ensuring that all children (in pairs) now have a 2×3 chocolate box and the right colours and number of sweets, Lisa now asks them how they are going to fit the chocolates in the box. Again, Lisa watches and listens, trying to notice the children who are showing an awareness of the next parameter of the problem: that same coloured sweets cannot go in adjacent slots. Once more, Lisa is seeking to create an opportunity to exemplify this parameter by drawing the children's attention to it. As part of this section the following dialogue takes place:

> Lisa: Ethan, tell me about the way you and Susie have been putting the sweets into your box?
> Ethan: Well we know that we can't have the mid grey ones next to each so we have spread them out.
> Lisa: What do you mean by 'spread them out'?'
> Ethan: Well if you put one [mid grey] here, then you can't put one [mid grey] here because that would be next to it. So the next one [mid grey] has to go in one of these spaces.
> Lisa (pointing back at the relevant 'rule' on the board): oh, because of this rule- you can't have two sweets of the same colour next to each other. Is diagonally okay? What does adjacent mean?

By questioning children like this and making links between their partial solutions and the listed parameters or rules on the board, Lisa is helping the children thoroughly understand the parameters of the investigation. This is a crucial step as you are aiming for all children to begin investigating a problem with a full understanding of the rules that they are investigating within.

> Lisa then waits and watches again until she sees a few pairs come up with solutions. Again, Lisa questions them to draw all children's attention to the parameters of the problem. How do you know this a solution? Does it keep to all of the rules? For each proposed solution, Lisa systematically tests it against each of the rules: a 2x3 box; 3 mid greys, 2 light greys and 1 dark grey; same colours cannot be in adjacent slots.

As we have spoken about previously, understanding the 'not' of a concept or rule further embeds a thorough understanding. Therefore Lisa now draws upon a possible solution which does not keep to the rules:

> Lisa: So this is my idea for a solution' [Lisa presents a solution with the correct box and sweets but with two mid greys touching each other.]

> *Lisa: Let's check, do I have a box with 2 rows of 3? Yes, okay, and do I have the right amount of sweets of the right colours?' [Lisa points to each of the sweets in her proposed solution to count the 3 mid greys, 2 light greys and 1 dark grey.]*
>
> *Lisa: Okay, so this works.*
>
> *Many of the children had already noticed that the solution broke rule three and were enthusiastically trying to say so while Lisa worked through the first two rules. By the time that Lisa exclaimed, 'Okay, so this works', most of the class were emphatically saying that it didn't work and explaining why. Lisa had successfully facilitated the children to notice for themselves what constituted a solution and what didn't; they now fully understood the parameters.*

As stated at the beginning of this case study, this is where this problem differs significantly from the coins-based problem; the parameters need to be explicitly explored and fully understood as opposed to being implicit through the coin values. When planning investigations such as these, do not underestimate the time and importance of this first part of the lesson.

> **Things to consider when introducing parameters of an investigation**
>
> - **Do not assume that the parameters and their significance are obvious to your children.**
> - **Plan carefully how you will introduce and explore each parameter.**
> - **Allow enough time for the children to notice the significance of the parameters for themselves.**
> - **Plan to explore 'non-solutions' as well as solutions to embed a thorough understanding of the parameters.**

Reasoning

So by this time, Lisa has supported the children to establish what qualifies as a solution and has a few possible solutions to the problem. Similar to Gareth, however, Lisa will now need to guide her children to think about this problem systematically. Again, however, Lisa is aiming to draw this systematic approach out of the children rather than simply tell them.

> Lisa gathers together the solutions from the whole group and poses the question, 'Are these all solutions? How do you know?' She then puts them alongside each other and asks the children if they notice anything.

Lisa is deliberately drawing the children's attention to how the parameters affect the solutions. Lisa asks the children 'why' and 'how do you know' throughout this analysis of the current solutions, constantly encouraging the children to draw on the established parameters.

Conjecturing

At one point a child, Tabitha, points to the solutions and exclaims that 'the mid greys have to go in a v or a hill'. (see Figure 6.3).

Figure 6.3

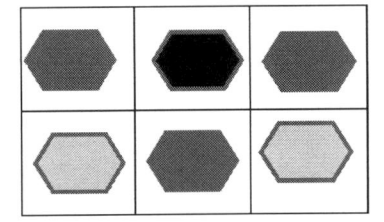

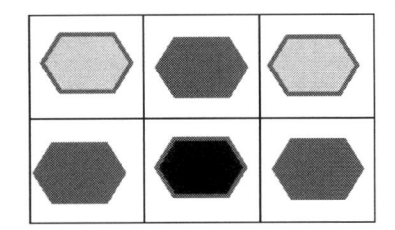

> Lisa, having done the investigation before the lesson, was looking out for this turning point in the children's thinking so she thanks Tabitha for her conjecture and asks her to explain more. Lisa carefully supports Tabitha to explain why this was the case, making links to the parameters of the problem.
>
> Similar to Gareth, Lisa is now faced with children arguing that these two solutions are in fact the same, and again, this gives Lisa an opportunity to explore the parameters further and suggest a possible refinement that the class agrees on. Giving children ownership at junctures like this is an underpinning step to supporting them to suggest their own parameters to problems.
>
> This turning point in the investigation is also the beginning of a systematic approach as all the solutions have to begin with either one of these patterns. We can now find all the solutions that begin with the first option and then find all the solutions that begin with the second option. The problem has become more manageable and can now be approached systematically.

Lisa now turns her attention to supporting the children to consider how to record their solutions. This is an important planning decision if your investigation begins with concrete resources as you need to consider how to move your children from exploring the resources to systematically using the resources whilst recording each solution that they find. As the systematic recording begins, some children may not need the resources anymore, but it is vital that all children are offered them at the exploration stage and can continue to use them. Again, Lisa wants this to be drawn from the children, so she has prepared both plain paper and squared paper. She takes ideas from children, modelling their explanations and making sure that all children are now in a position to investigate the problem themselves.

Exploring further
Rich Tweak 6.6 – Adapting the parameters; encouraging 'what-ifs'

As spoken about at the beginning of this chapter and mentioned in Case Study 6.1, encouraging children to extend an investigation by asking 'what if' questions is an extremely powerful way of engaging children in the process of the investigation and further developing their mathematical thinking. However, children's learning needs to be scaffolded in order to be successful in this process. For example, if a child decided to explore a 'what if' that involved a chocolate box that was enormous, the investigation would quickly become overwhelming and the underlying mathematics would be lost. The power of explicitly exploring the parameters of investigations is that we can then encourage them to adapt the investigation by changing only one of the parameters. Using this approach, the following, more manageable 'what ifs' could emerge:

What if the chocolate box was 1×6?
What if there are 2 of each colour of sweet?
What if there are 12 sweets in a 2×6 sweet box but the ratios of the sweets are the same?
What if there are only two colours with 3 of each?

These 'what ifs' illustrate the beauty of investigations, because they can continue to be explored. Adapting the ratios of the sweets or looking at a 2×6 box, then a 2×9 box and so on. For example, might generate a pattern related to the number of possible solutions each time? As children pose their 'what ifs', they can be encouraged to conjecture what might happen. For example, will a 2×6 box with the same ratio of sweets have twice as many solutions? In this way, we can also see how a simple investigation that is accessible for younger children could be used with older children, where the initial problem is quickly explored before spending more time exploring 'what ifs'.

Activity ideas and their rich tweaks

Rich Tweaks	
Standard Activity	**Rich Tweak Activity**
Identify odd and even numbers	Does an odd number plus and odd number make another add number? What about odd + even? What about even + even? What if we multiply odds and evens?
Joe throws three bean bags into three buckets marked with either a 1, 2 or 3. What is his score if he got all three beanbags into the bucket marked 2?	If all Joe's bean bags land in a bucket, what is the highest/lowest possible score that he could have got? Can you find all the possible scores for Joe? What would the possible scores be if he only got two beanbags in the bucket? Four beanbags in the buckets?
Number calculations with the four operations	Can you make the numbers 1 to 12 using only the digits 1, 2, 3 and 4 and any of the four operations (e.g. 4 × 2 + 1 = 9) Which solutions can you use again and adapt to find out how to make a different number (e.g. 4 + 2 = 6 so 4 + 2 × 2 = 12) When I roll my 4 dice, I get a total of 18. Which numbers did I roll? How many different ways to do this can you find? I have 15 books that I want to share out between 3 tables. How many books could I put on each table? How many different ways to do this can you find?

What is the value of each digit in the Hundreds, Tens, Ones (HTO). Tenths (TH) grid?	Finding palindromic numbers (i.e. those which read the same forwards and backwards such as 252) How many palindromic numbers are there between 0 and 100? 100 and 200? 0 and 1000? 1000 and 1100? Or between 1 and 10 (to include decimals)?
Finding the difference between numbers (e.g. what is the difference between 4 and 15?)	Which two numbers could I add to 4 to give me a total of 15?
Divide a square in half	How many different ways of dividing a square in half can you find?
Properties of shapes – what are the properties of a regular pentagon?	How many different shapes can you make with 5 sticks? (Children can select sticks of different lengths.) How do the properties of these shapes differ from each other?
Shrinking Squares – Write a number in each corner of a square then calculate the difference between the numbers, writing this in the middle of each side. This allows you to draw another square in the middle and continue. . . . The squares finish when you get 0-0-0-0.	
	How does changing the numbers that you start with affect how many squares you get before reaching 0, 0, 0, 0? Why? What happens if you use consecutive numbers, 2-digit numbers, 3 digit numbers, odds only, evens, only, square numbers only etc What if you start with a triangle? Or a pentagon? Or a hexagon?

Investigations and systematic thinking ◆ 129

Pyramids	What do you notice? Does it matter what order the three numbers at the bottom are? Why?
– Put the numbers 1, 2 and 3 in any order in the bottom 3 squares. Write the sum of the underneath two squares in the next square up. Continue until you reach the top.	What if you could use each number multiple times on the bottom row? What if you use 2, 3, 4? Or 4, 5, 6? Or any other combination of three consecutive numbers? What if you started with four boxes on the bottom row? What if you found the product of the two numbers below rather than the sum?

Remember to always 'do' the investigation yourself before you use it in a lesson. This way, you are more prepared for the ideas that children may have and are better able to plan a 'journey' through the investigation in which the children feel autonomous.

References

Barclay, N. and Barnes, A. (2013) Big mathematical ideas-an idea with primary potential? *Mathematics Teaching: Journal of the Association of Teachers of Mathematics*, 234, pp. 19–21.

Boaler, J. (2009) *The Elephant in the Classroom*. London: Souvenir Press.

Nrich. (2011) *Creating a Low Threshold High Ceiling Classroom*. Available from: maths.org (Accessed: 9 December 2020).

Nrich. (2013) *Low Threshold High Ceiling – An Introduction*. Available from: https://nrich.maths.org/10345 (Accessed: 29 October 2020).

7
Planning for mathematical thinking

In this, the final chapter of the book, we think about how you can plan lessons which give children opportunities for the kinds of mathematical thinking we have been discussing. Each of the previous chapters has looked at an aspect of mathematical thinking and offered some specific examples of 'rich tweaks', which enhance the opportunities for mathematical thinking. In order to be illustrative, these examples have been specific, set in the context of specific lessons, or case studies. In this chapter, we offer you some more general thoughts, which we hope you will be able to apply to any lesson or sequence of lessons that you are planning. These are not intended to be used as a rigid checklist that must be incorporated into every lesson. However, we do suggest that you keep some of these thoughts close to your planning folder so that you can draw on them when you are planning a lesson or sequence of lessons in which you are trying to develop the children's mathematical thinking.

In the first part of the chapter, we explore some general thoughts about planning, which can be applied to any mathematical topic. In the second part of the chapter, we try to exemplify these so that you can apply the principles to your own planning.

Planning for mathematical thinking

Witt (2014) is very clear that good planning involves clarity of thought about what we want the children to learn. As you plan lessons that are intended to develop your children's mathematical thinking, try to be very clear about which aspect of mathematical thinking your lessons are designed to develop. Hazy, unformed thoughts about simply developing the children's mathematical thinking are less likely to result in the kinds of focused activities that will be effective.

In seeking to plan for mathematical thinking, we look at some of the 'rich tweaks' that have been presented so far and explore what they have in common. In this way, some general principles for planning might become clear. In this section, we also refer to the mastery assessment documents of the National Centre of Excellence for Teaching Mathematics (NCETM), which contain useful information about the 'markers of mastery', that is learning behaviours which indicate that a child has understood a topic deeply. We consider each of them in turn.

According to the NCETM (Askew et al., 2015), a pupil really understands a mathematical concept, idea or technique if they can describe it in their own words.

Learners of foreign languages know that vocabulary can be passive or active. *Passive vocabulary* refers to words that a learner can understand but cannot yet use. *Active vocabulary*, on the other hand, is vocabulary that can be both understood and generated by the speaker. Learning (mathematical learning in particular) works in a very similar way; some learners will be able to understand a concept when it is explained to them but will be unable to then use that idea themselves. Shimamura (2018) suggests that learning is a generative activity, that is that for effective learning to take place, learners need to produce something rather than simply be passive recipients of knowledge. To achieve the deep learning that is envisaged by the 'mastery' approach to teaching mathematics, it is important that learners attain an active understanding of concepts, that is an understanding that enables them to use their knowledge.

There is a saying that 'teaching is a second learning', and the benefits of teaching something on the teacher's understanding have been long recognised (see Cohen, Kulik and Kulik, 1982, for a summary). A more recent study by Koh et al. (2018) has suggested that these benefits may arise due to the teacher having to retrieve knowledge before teaching it. The benefits of retrieval on learning are also widely documented (see Rosenshine, 2012). Fiorella and Mayer (2016) suggest eight strategies that can transform passive learning experiences into more active ones, enabling children to develop an active understanding of concepts.

These studies all relate clearly to the NCETM's assertion that a deep understanding of a mathematical concept or technique is shown when a pupil is able to explain it in their own words.

As you plan your mathematics lessons, you should plan opportunities for the children to explain their mathematical understanding, both to you (the teacher) and to each other.

Being asked to explain their understanding will encourage them to retrieve knowledge and to organise it in a clear and logical way. This may well also expose areas where they (and you) had thought that understanding was stronger than it is. Opportunities for this kind of explanation can be incorporated into lessons relatively easily; the children can work in pairs or trios for a few minutes where one child takes on the role of teacher and explains to their peers. The others can ask questions or support if the 'teacher' (i.e. the child giving the explanation) has an incomplete understanding or has failed to explain a concept clearly. It is also important that you (the teacher) acquire the habit of asking children to explain an answer rather than simply accepting a single word answer. So, as you plan, try to ensure that your children's mathematical learning involves the generation of something, ideally a verbal or written explanation of their understanding.

According to the NCETM, a pupil really understands a mathematical concept, idea or technique if he or she can represent it in a variety of ways (e.g. using concrete materials, pictures and symbols – the Concrete–Pictorial–Abstract [CPA] approach). It is well beyond the scope of this chapter to provide a detailed discussion of the CPA approach to teaching maths. If this is something that you are unfamiliar with, we suggest that you look at some of the many explanations that are available, for example the Third Space Learning discussion available at https://thirdspacelearning.com/blog/concrete-pictorial-abstract-maths-cpa/.

In the preceding section, we noted the fact that learners generating an explanation of their understanding triggers retrieval, which has been shown many times to deepen understanding (Karpicke and Roediger, 2008). Depth of understanding can also be demonstrated by representing ideas in multiple ways, not just verbally and using mathematical symbols.

> **As you plan, we recommend that you try to incorporate into your lessons opportunities for children to illustrate and represent their understanding in a range of ways. This may involve using concrete manipulative objects such as Cuisenaire rods or Dienes blocks and asking the children to use them to represent or demonstrate their thinking.**

There is a temptation to think that the CPA approach means that children should move from the concrete to the pictorial and finally to the abstract. While it is certainly the case that, for the vast majority of children, concrete representations of mathematical concepts are easier to grasp than abstract ones; it is not the case that concrete or pictorial representations are merely stepping-stones to more abstract ones. We recommend that you plan so that your children have opportunities to move between all these different representations. For example, you might give them a calculation in its abstract form (7 + 6) and ask them to represent this using Dienes blocks or to draw a picture. You might give the children a picture and ask them to represent what is happening mathematically using concrete resources and abstract symbols.

Activity – Have a go at this yourself. Following are a couple of abstract representations of calculations, or situations. Spend a couple of minutes, exploring physical (concrete) and pictorial representations of them.

4 + 7 = 11
1/4 of 12
11 – 7 = 4

According to the NCETM, a pupil really understands a mathematical concept, idea or technique if they can make up their own examples (and non-examples) of it. As a teacher, you will be thinking carefully about the examples that you use to ensure that they illustrate the specific mathematical concept that you want your learners to pay attention to. You may also make use of non-examples as a way of focusing children's attention on the important aspects of a concept, or technique.

For example, you may give children examples of subtraction questions which do not need any re-arranging (or decomposition) and then some which do. Asking the children what is the same and what is different about the questions helps to draw their attention to this key difference.

As you plan, try to incorporate into your lesson plans time for the children to make up their own examples (and non-examples).

This could be calculations, or shapes, or ways of representing data. All aspects of mathematical learning can be explored from this point of view. To help you develop this part of your planning, you might want to consider the following areas of maths and construct an example and a non-example of each one:

1. A subtraction calculation that involves re-arranging (decomposition)
2. A pentagon with two right angles

3   A data set where the mean and median are the same
4   A distance that is 5 km when measured to the nearest 100 m
5   Two numbers with a difference of 3.5

As you may have realised from trying this exercise, thinking of specific examples is quite demanding mathematically and involves a deeper level of thinking than simply recognising something (e.g. a shape) or carrying out a calculation.

Asking children to generate non-examples can be equally powerful. For example, you may ask your children to come up with a subtraction calculation, which involves 're-arranging' from the tens to the ones but not from the hundreds to the tens or a quadrilateral shape with no right angles.

As you plan lessons, it would be good to sprinkle in opportunities for the children to generate their own examples. As with many of these suggestions, doing this will also offer you an insight into the depth of each child's mathematical thinking. You may find that you have children who are able to carry out specific processes relatively fluently but who struggle to come up with specific examples to illustrate those processes.

Again, according to the NCETM documentation, a child really understands a concept or technique if they can recognise it in new situations and contexts. Mathematical thinking involves being able to see beyond the surface features of a mathematical idea to the underlying mathematics. Barton (2018) talks about problems having the same surface but different depth (SSDD). There is a whole website of such problems (https://ssddproblems.com/). He recommends presenting learners with a range of problems, which superficially appear to be about the same thing but which contain different mathematics.

For example, have a look the following two problems.

> John and Steve each have some pencils. John has 6 pencils and Steve has 7 pencils. How many pencils do they have in total?

John and Steve each have 6 packets of pencils. There are 7 pencils in each packet. How many pencils do they have in total?

Children might look at these two questions and conclude that they are very similar to each other. They are both about John and Steve, they are both about pencils and they even contain the same numbers (6 and 7). However, mathematically they are very different; one is an additive problem and one is multiplicative. Planning opportunities for children to explore (and possibly sort – see the following discussion) different problems will help them develop the skill in seeing beyond the surface of the problem to the underlying maths.

Give it a try.

Let's imagine that you are working in Year 3 and are coming to the end of a series of lessons on calculation and problem-solving. Pause at this point and see if you can write two different word problems which have a similar surface but which require different mathematical operations. Try to write two problems with the same surface, one of which requires subtraction and one of which involves division.

Some of these different planning strategies seem to overlap. For example, planning opportunities for children to tackle SSDD problems can be further expanded by encouraging the children to come up with their own examples of SSDD problems.

Related to the above discussion is the NCETM's contention that learners who have really understood a concept or technique are able to see connections between it and other facts or ideas and to apply it to new situations. As you plan, it would be good to consider how you might help children to make links between the mathematics they are studying, and other areas of mathematics. Skilful maths teachers can use the examples they choose (or the problems they set) as a way of nudging children towards greater understanding.

For example, here are two seemingly unrelated problems:

Coloured pencils are sold in packets of 8. Mr Generous wants to buy a packet of coloured pencils for each of the 32 children in his class. How many pencils will he buy?

Farmer Palmer has a field, which is 100 m long and 30 m wide. What is the area of his field?

Some children may immediately see that the two problems involve multiplication but may only know this because they have been told and remembered that finding the area of rectangles involves multiplication. Putting the two problems next to each other and asking the children to identify what is the same about them (beyond the fact that they both involve multiplication) may help them understand more deeply why finding the area of a rectangle requires multiplication.

So, as you plan your lessons, it may be worth planning examples that are connected but where the connection is not obvious.

Before we move on, we suggest that you might add a third problem to the preceding two:

Farmer Giles has a field which is 120 m long, but only 20 m wide. He wants to put a fence around it. How many metres of fencing does he need?

You might then invite the children to look at those three problems and decide which is the odd one out. Superficially, the question about the coloured pencils is the odd one out, as it involves pencils and the other two involve farmers. However, a deeper look at the mathematical structure of the questions makes it clear that the final problem is mathematically different from the other two. To reinforce the point about combining these strategies, asking the children to write three problems for their peers, one of which is the 'odd one out' can be a powerful strategy to incorporate into your planning.

Finally in this section, we note that the NCETM's mastery assessment documentation says that a child understands a specific concept, or technique at greater depth, if they can independently explore and investigate mathematical contexts and structures, communicate results clearly and systematically explain and generalise the mathematics.

We hope that the chapters about systematic thinking (Chapter 6) and about generalising (Chapter 5) will have given you good ideas about how to plan for this. We end this section with a thought about mathematical communication.

Consider planning opportunities for the children to communicate their understanding clearly and systematically.

Bahir (2014) provides some interesting ideas about encouraging children to communicate their mathematical understanding including the use of a jotter to make informal notes and a book of more formal mathematical communication. For example, at the end of a unit of work on adding fractions, the children might be encouraged to take two pages in their book and use a combination of written words, diagrams, examples, pictures and the like to explain what they have learned. Similarly, after some lessons in which the children have been taught how to use a protractor, they might work in pairs to produce a leaflet explaining how to use a protractor. We should emphasise here that this is done at the end of a sequence of lessons. Inevitably, the children will pay some attention to the leaflet's design (getting the font right, etc.) and therefore not to the mathematics. This is inevitable, so it is important to set clear success criteria for the leaflet that are related to mathematics.

If we consider Case Study 3.3, it seems clear that the tweak that turned a routine question into one that involved more reasoning and a greater depth of thinking was one of the question having more than one answer. This may be a useful guiding principle as you seek to plan lessons that develop mathematical thinking.

As you plan, consider ways to tweak a problem, or calculation, so that it has more than one correct answer.

Give it a try:

While you consider the idea of tweaking questions so that they have more than one answer, here are a few examples for you to try (with our suggestions that follow). Before you look at our suggestions, take a couple of minutes and see if you can apply a 'rich tweak' to each of these questions so that it now has more than one answer:

1. What is the area of a rectangle with sides 5 m, 5 m, 4 m and 4 m?
2. What is 83 ÷ 3?
3. What is the mean average of this set of scores: 12, 17, 15, 16, 10, 20, 22?
4. What is the difference between 1/3 and 1/2?

Here are our suggestions:

1. Draw two different rectangles with an area of 20 m²?
2. Find three division calculations where the divisor is 3 and the remainder is 2.
3. Find two sets of 7 scores where the mean average is 16.
4. Find two fractions which have a difference of less than 1/4.

In helping you to plan for these kinds of questions, we strongly recommend you look at the Open Middle website (see Chapter 2 for more on this).

One of the things we particularly like about this tweak in the planning is the fact that it gives more choice and agency to the children. Our final thought in this section, to help guide your planning is that you consider ways to give the children more control over their mathematics. This may take the form of the children making their own questions or examples. It may come in the form of them choosing how to approach a problem or how to communicate or represent their thinking.

To summarise our thoughts so far, as you plan, we recommend the following:

- Plan opportunities for the children to explain their mathematical understanding, both to you (the teacher) and to each other.
- Try to incorporate into your lessons opportunities for children to illustrate and represent their understanding in a range of ways.
- Try to incorporate opportunities for the children to make up their own examples (and non-examples) and questions.
- Allow children to see and work with examples and questions that are connected but where the connection is not obvious.
- Create opportunities for the children to communicate their understanding clearly and systematically.
- Consider ways to tweak a problem, or calculation so that it has more than one correct answer.

References

Askew, M., Morgan, D., Griffin, P., Bishop, S., Eaton, S. and Christie, C. (2015) *Teaching for Mastery: Questions, Tasks and Activities to Support Assessment*. Oxford University Press. Available from: www.ncetm.org.uk/classroom-resources/assessment-materials-primary/ (Accessed: 21 September 2020).

Bahir. (2014) Communicating mathematically. In M. Witt (ed.), *Primary Mathematics for Trainee Teachers*. London: Sage.

Barton, C. (2018) *How I Wish I'd Taught Maths*. Woodbridge: John Catt Educational.

Cohen, P. A., Kulik, J. A. and Kulik, C. L. C. (1982) Educational outcomes of tutoring: A meta-analysis of findings. *American Educational Research Journal*, 19(2), pp. 237–248.

Fiorella, L. and Mayer, R. E. (2016) Eight ways to promote generative learning. *Educational Psychology Review*, 28(4), pp. 717–741.

Karpicke, J. D. and Roediger, H. L. (2008) The critical importance of retrieval for learning. *Science*, 319(5865), pp. 966–968.

Koh, A. W. L., Lee, S. C. and Lim, S. W. H. (2018) The learning benefits of teaching: A retrieval practice hypothesis. *Applied Cognitive Psychology*, 32(3), pp. 401–410.

Rosenshine, B. (2012) Principles of instruction: Research-based strategies that all teachers should know. *American Educator*, 36(1), p. 12.

Shimamura, A. (2018) *MARGE a Whole Brain Learning Approach for Students and Teachers*. Available from: https://shimamurapubs.files.wordpress.com/2018/09/marge_shimamura.pdf (Accessed: 3 September 2020).

Witt, M. (2014) *Primary Mathematics for Trainee Teachers*. London: Sage.

Conclusion

We hope that you have enjoyed the book, whether you have read it sequentially or whether you have dipped into different chapters. We hope that the chapters have given you a host of ideas for enriching your own maths lessons.

We believe that there is a great deal more to maths than simply performing calculations. Being an outstanding maths teacher should involve having a broad vision for what mathematics involves. Embracing this vision is not especially easy. It is probably easier to simply follow a scheme (if your school is using one) and have your children work through several examples until they are confident and competent with a particular algorithm or process. The fact that you have read this book suggests that you feel (as we do) that this is not enough to give the children you teach a high-quality maths education.

At the moment, incorporating more opportunities for your children to engage in mathematical thinking may seem like a daunting undertaking. Allowing the children some freedom to engage in mathematical thinking may involve them taking the maths in directions that you hadn't anticipated. You may have a group of children whose experiences of maths lessons have exclusively been copying a process modelled to them by the teacher. They may not know how to react when presented with opportunities to engage in mathematical thinking; it may seem daunting to them as well.

If that is the case, we would encourage you not to give up, but maybe to start in a small way, one that feels comfortable for both you and the children. For example, you might try giving them an 'odd one out' question (see Chapter 3). One of the advantages of this activity is that there is more than one answer. On one level, this is very helpful for encouraging mathematical thinking; the children are not all trying to guess what is in the teacher's head.

This increases the scope for more interesting mathematical thinking. A second advantage of this activity is that it helps to instil in the children the idea that mathematical questions can have more than one answer and that the process of doing mathematics involves more than copying an example that the teacher has given or trying to arrive at the single, accepted, 'correct' answer to a given question.

So, we hope that this book, and the ideas contained in it, will help not only to offer the children you teach a richer and more varied mathematical experience but also will support you in developing a classroom ethos where questioning, offering answers, exploring patterns and possibilities, making conjectures and testing them out and engaging in mathematical reasoning are the rule rather than the exception in maths lessons. We hope that you will begin to build a 'psychological environment' in your classroom where the children become happy to ask their own questions, offer mathematical opinions and think mathematically. We appreciate that this is a high ideal and that it is much easier said than done. That said, we feel that it is by no means impossible and that it is much better to try to achieve some success than not to try at all. We hope that this book will play a role in helping you to achieve this environment for your children and we wish you every success in your teaching.

Fay, Amanda and Marcus
The University of the West
of England Primary Mathematics Team

Index

Page numbers in *italics* indicate a figure on the corresponding page.

abstract calculation 2
abstract symbols 25, 35
acceleration, through curriculum 11
active real-life context problems 63
active vocabulary 132
addition 25, 27, 30, 69, 80–81, 99, 104
Advisory Committee on Mathematics Education 8
Ahmed, A. 80
angles, rich tweaks 57
area: and perimeter 53–56; rich tweaks 60

Back, J. 16
Bahir 139
Barclay, N. 3, 14–15, 117
bar models 79
Barnes, A. 3, 14–15, 117
Barton, C. 33, 50, 74, 136
big and small numbers 73
Big Ideas 3, 14, 15
Boaler, J. 64, 82
Burns, M. 85

calculations 2
Christodoulou, D. 22
coherence 9
communication 15
competence 109
Concrete–Pictorial–Abstract (CPA) approach 134
conjecturing 125–126
curriculum National Curriculum for Mathematics

De Corte, E. 71
deep understanding, of mathematical concept 11, 133
degree of fluency 26–27
digit cards 38
divergent thinking 15
division 25, 81, 104, 137, 140
Drury, H. 11

Early Career Teachers (ECT) 1
equal sign 25, 27
equivalence 15
estimation and reasoning 67
Even Better Maths (Ahmed and Williams) 80
exploring 117–118

factors, rich tweaks 105
Fermi, E. 67
Fermi questions 66–68
Fiorella, L. 133
fluency 8, 10
foreign languages, learners of 132
fractions, comparing 38
function machines 35–38

generality 15
geometry and statistics 2–3; logical thinking 42; reasoning in 41–56; rich tweaks 31–57; shape reveal activities 43–48
goal-free problems 50, 74
graphs 50–52

growing patterns 91
'Guess the Shape' 43–48

Haylock, D. 15, 25, 42
Higgins, S. 65

input–output analysis 36
investigative mathematical thinking 109–113; finding all the possibilities 114–115; recording children's thinking 113–130; systematic thinking 109

Johnson-Wilder, S. 12

Kaplinsky, R. 33
Koh, A. W. L. 133

Lee, C. 12
length, rich tweaks 69–72
Liljedahl, P. 89
logical thinking 42
logic and proof 15
low threshold, high ceiling (LTHC) tasks 12, 85, 110

magic V problem 95–96
manipulation of model 71
Mason, J. 103
mastery: markers of 10, 132; principles 9–12
mathematical development 21
mathematical operations 36; addition 25, 27, 30, 69, 80–81, 99, 104; division 25, 81, 104, 137, 140; multiplication 25, 31, 79, 81, 99–100, 104, 138; subtraction 25, 27, 30, 69, 80–81, 104, 135–137
mathematical reasoning 21–38, 41–61; see also reasoning; reasoning through calculation
mathematical thinking 1–2, 10, 127, 143; development of 110; embedding into lessons 16–18; ideas of 3; learners 14; opportunities 37; planning for 131–141; see also Big Ideas; rich tweaks
Maths Hubs 9
Mayer, R. E. 133
measures (weight), rich tweaks 60
multi-digit calculations 26–27
multiplication 25, 31, 79, 81, 99–100, 104, 138

National Centre for Excellence in the Teaching of Mathematics (NCETM) 9–10, 132, 136
National Curriculum for Mathematics 21–22, 69, 86; document 34; for primary mathematics 1, 8, 10–11, 16
noticing 100–102, 122–124
Nrich 12–13, 15, 76, 109–110
number chains 114
numerical sequence 92
Nunes, T. 21, 32
nutrition, human 16

odd and even numbers, rich tweaks 128
Open Middle problems 33–37

Papic, M. 103
parallel lines 47
passive vocabulary 132
patterns: exploration of 85; and structure 14
patterns and variation 85–86; generalising, to support 94–99; procedural variation 99–103; repeating and growing patterns 86–94
perimeter, rich tweaks 60; see also area, and perimeter
Piggot, J. 76
practice-and-drill approach 64
pre-service (trainee) teachers 1
primary mathematics teaching 7; 'Big ideas' 14–15; depth 11; Ideas to help solve 'the problem' 12–14;

mastery 9–11; mathematical thinking into lessons 16–18
Primary National Curriculum for Mathematics 7
problem-solving 2–3, 8, 63–65; closing questions 77; degree of emphasis 64; difference 66; environment 76; point 66; questioning to support and scaffold 73–82; rich tweaks 82–83, 105; RUCSAC and other directions 68–73; seeing and doing 65–68; writing word problems 78
procedural variation 99–103
Programme of International Student Assessment (PISA) 9
proof, logic and 15

questioning strategies 74–82

real-life (or pseudo-real-life) problems 63
reasoning 8, 42, 44, 98–99, 102–103, 125; about area and perimeter 53–56; about shapes 43–49; about statistics 49–53; finding all possibilities 115–117
reasoning through calculation 21–22; developments in reasoning in calculation 27–31; function machines 34–37; position of unknown in calculation questions 22–24, *23*; reasoning from given calculation 31–33; reasoning using equality symbol *24*, 24–25; Robert Kaplinsky's 'open middle' problems 33–34; varying the unknown in formal written calculations 25–27
recording thinking 113–130
regular and irregular shapes, rich tweaks 59
repeating patterns, rich tweaks *88*, 88–89
representation 15; fluency 10; mathematical concepts 134; of multiplication 81; physical and pictorial 135; and structure 9
resilience 15
rich tweaks 2, 4, 21; activity ideas and 128–130; adapting the parameters 127; angles 57; area 60; arranging chocolates 121–122; big and small numbers 73; calculation strategies 30–31, 38; children's own questions about an investigation 111–112; conjecturing/explaining 97–98; developments in reasoning in calculation 27–31; encouraging 'what-ifs' 127; exploring/noticing/conjecturing 96–97; factors 105; Fermi questions 66–68; fractions 106; geometry and statistics 31–57; length 69–72; measures 60; noticing/conjecturing 91–94; number calculations 128; odd and even numbers 128; operations 104; patterns in solutions 96–97; patterns to predict 102; perimeter 60; position of unknown in calculation questions 22–24, *23*; problem-solving 82–83, 105; procedural variation 100; pyramids 130; reasoning from given calculation 31–33; reasoning using equality symbol *24*, 24–25; regular and irregular shapes 59; repeating patterns *88*, 88–91; shapes, properties of 58–61, 129; squares, shrinking 129; statistics 57; tessellation/capacity 58; time 60; transferring thinking 98; varying the unknown in formal written calculations 25–27; 'what happens if. . . ?' questions 112–113; writing word problems 78
RUCSAC (**R**ead the question, **U**nderline the key information, **C**hoose the operation, **S**olve the problem, **A**nswer the question, **C**heck your answer) 68–73

same surface but different depth (SSDD) 136–137
scaling multiplication 91
shapes: properties of 43–49, 58–61; reveal activities 42–49; rich tweaks 58–61, 129
Shimamura, A. 132
Skemp, R. 24
small numbers, and big numbers 73
statistics: reasoning about 49–53; rich tweaks 57; *see also* geometry and statistics
subtraction 25, 27, 30, 69, 80–81, 104, 135–137
successive terms *87*
surveys 49
systematic thinking 109

teaching calculations 2
Tessellation/capacity 57
three-digit formal calculations 28
Threlfall, J. 103
time, rich tweaks 60

unknown, varying position in calculations 38

variation 10
Verschaffel, L. 71

Watson, A. 103
Williams, H. 80
Witt, M. 131–132
word problems, writing 78

Printed in Great Britain
by Amazon